THE CONFIDENT BODY

THE CONFIDENT BODY

A FUNCTIONAL APPROACH TO
UNLOCKING YOUR FULL POTENTIAL

MINNA TAYLOR

NEW DEGREE PRESS
COPYRIGHT © 2022 MINNA TAYLOR
All rights reserved.

THE CONFIDENT BODY
A Functional Approach to Unlocking Your Full Potential

ISBN	979-8-88504-129-4	*Paperback*
	979-8-88504-759-3	*Kindle Ebook*
	979-8-88504-238-3	*Ebook*

Contents

WELCOME	7
LEARN	**15**
UNCONSCIOUS CONDITIONING	17
OBSERVATION	33
NOW YOU SEE IT	45
STATUS AND POWER	53
WHAT IS POSSIBLE	65
IMAGINE	**75**
BENEFITS OF DISCOMFORT	77
TRUTH TELLING	85
INEVITABLE VULNERABILITY	97
BODY AND BREATH	109
AWARENESS	119
PLAY	**129**
DIRECTING THE BODY	131
MOVEMENT AND VIBRATION	147
PLAYFUL PRACTICE	171
A PLAYFUL LIFE	185

CONCLUSION	**199**
NO DUMB QUESTIONS	201
ACKNOWLEDGMENTS	**211**
APPENDIX	**217**

Welcome

I am currently coming at you from my 300-square-foot studio in Brooklyn, New York. I bought my apartment three months prior to the pandemic, so, unlike many of my friends, I couldn't abandon ship and move home or to some tropical paradise. I have a mortgage now. I am aware how concrete that statement sounds, immovable in its philosophy, implying that a mortgage somehow correlates to staying put. Neither here nor there. I spend a lot of time alone anyway, but particularly these days. These are the pandemic days. Like many of my fellow single humans, I have developed an intimate relationship with Netflix. I'd like to tell you I have spent my screen time wisely, absorbing an abundance of edifying content, but I would be lying. It's 90 percent mindless garbage.

So here I am, watching *The Circle*, a competition reality show about people locked in their own tiny apartments interacting with the other contestants through a make-shift social media platform. I'm watching the first episode where they are introducing the characters, and the first guy to be introduced is big and bold. He wears a tight shirt and has an earring dangling from his right ear in the shape of a cross. He tells us about himself and his myriad positive qualities and then divulges his strategy for gaining the loyalty of the other contestants to ultimately win top influencer status. (I told you it was garbage.) He outlines the secret as: "eye contact and confidence. If you have confidence, the ladies will love you." (The Circle, 2020)

Ignoring the gag-worthy button to that award-winning strategy, I couldn't help but wonder, "What the hell is he talking about?" What does he actually mean when he says, "Have confidence"?

I'm sure you hear this all the time. Like, "Oh yeah, just have confidence in yourself; just be confident." But do you ever take the time to really break down what that means? Amy Cuddy, author of *Presence*, writes about it in terms of "powerful poses" versus "powerless poses," or we hear Brené Brown, best known for her work on vulnerability, talk about grounded confidence as "the messy process of learning and unlearning, practicing and failing, and surviving misses." (Brown, 2018) Now I adore these women. I consider them colleagues in the field of personal development and value their research and contributions to the study of human behavior, but I am still left with the question. Fundamentally, and at a purely functional, physical level, what are we talking about? How do we understand, practice, and develop confidence?

I want you to think about this book as an initial kick-start, building a foundation, and consistent future access point of skills, mindset, and practices that will set you up for a lifetime of development, exploration, and embodiment of confidence. It is a lifelong practice. Just as you evolve, so must your confidence journey. It is not static. It is not a "Learn, Do, Done" process. If you are seeking sincere transformation, you have come to the right place.

Everything you seek to become is already inside of you. It's just buried under a pile of unnecessary junk. For example, my junk is wrapped up in the fact that I am an identical twin. We're not at the level of identical where we could pull off a Parent Trap situation, but we're clearly alike. We refer to it simply as "same egg, different people." When we were born, I was a full pound larger than her, and that differential has maintained itself throughout our development. I always knew I was slightly larger but didn't necessarily have an association for it beyond a data point during our annual physical. Then one day in second grade, the class was getting settled in a circle for show and tell, when some kid declares from across the circle that I am the fat twin. Suddenly I was bestowed an identity, a label. Not only was I "the fat twin," but I had another human as a glaring, unrelenting example of what it would look like to be the thin twin.

From that point on, it was a slow and steady escalation of compounding insecurity. My mom was constantly dieting, so I became aware of nutrition as a fat versus thin decision. It was the rise of the MTV generation, so the notion of image and celebrity was merging into a relationship with a toxic diet culture fueled by Crystal Pepsi, Olestra, and the Atkins miracle cure. I developed dominating vocal habits and a broad humor to distract from my self-consciousness about my body. I, like so many women, learned to hold in my stomach. I would walk with this crazy right leg movement to ensure that my thighs didn't rub together when I walked (rubbing thighs is totally freaking normal, by the way!). This misaligned relationship to my body simply amplified and reinforced a misalignment in my body itself.

This followed me into college. When I first started at NYU Tisch for acting, I would perform a scene in class and my unconscious habit was to cross my right arm in front of my stomach and land it in the elbow's crook of the left arm, leaving me closed off and only able to gesture with my left forearm. It was a mess, and I was totally unaware! It was self-conscious faux art. I was so aware of being watched and evaluated. I was coming from a farm in Appalachia and performing with kids who grew up as child actors in LA. I was so out of my element. I didn't want to be seen, but I had no choice. So, I did what felt safe. I crossed my arms in the most uninspired way possible. At least, that is how it started. Gradually, I began to love moving my body. I loved the feeling of permission to release the impulse of expression. To gesture. To feel an intention so fully that it had to be released in unanticipated movement—the flick of a hand, the wink of an eye, the tapping of a foot. I learned to connect deeply to my breath and share full, warm, dynamic vibration. To play the music of my thoughts. This doesn't mean I loved my body and had worked through the psychological milestones to forgive my younger self. In fact, I developed such a deep relationship with the potential of my body that I didn't have space for my relationship to the limitations or inadequacies of my body. I didn't spend energy trying to fix myself. I simply engaged in the practices I was taught that would lead to my incremental transformation. I investigated the acts of stillness and running in silence. I became obsessed with the phonetic movement of sounds in the mouth. I focused on what my voice felt like as it moved through my body and out into the world.

By the end of my first year, I had eliminated my southern accent and dropped the pitch of my voice significantly. I was moving freely during my scene work—no more bizarre, crossed arm situations. I addressed all the habits that were undermining my desire to be at ease and playful and authentic. I did this not by trying to get rid of them, but by dedicating my primary focus to exploring new habits. Those are the ones that stuck. One plus one equals two. Who I am today is not an accident. I was cultivated over years of consistent and continuous practice of both mind and body. We are all capable of living in a confident body.

This book will take a functional approach to unlocking your full potential. I believe that in order to move beyond the junk that holds us hostage in our minds, we must reconnect to the body. Our beliefs, our behaviors, our capability are deeply rooted in the fabric of our being, or rather, the fascia of our being. By placing the focus on our bodies, we bypass the attachment to the blockers of the mind. That voice that says, "You can't." That narrative that repeats "Don't bother." Exploring the breath functionally, for example, requires no psychological permission. It's just a matter of opening breath, ribs, intercostal muscles, tongue, larynx. And it will transform your life. You will feel space between reaction and response. You will have a deeper level of ease in those uneasy moments. You will speak your truth even when you aren't certain exactly what to say. You will embrace your feelings while not holding them as facts. Your life will be just as challenging, but it will no longer feel difficult. You will surrender your identity of suffering.

This book is for you, the high performer at any stage in your life or career, looking to harness authentic habits that will catapult you across the threshold of fear and usher you into a life of boldness, surrender, and truly embodied confidence. I am certain you have your own junk that has shaped your behavior and held you back from crossing the threshold. I have worked with leaders of multinational organizations, leading global teams, and responsible for millions of dollars in business units, express their fear of not being accepted and approved by their teams. I have watched Ivy League-educated senior executives fear screwing up. I have watched women leaders around the world resign themselves to a system not designed for them and reflect that on their own value as powerful contributors to their organizations. I have seen various systems erode confidence at every level, and I can tell you the solution is simpler than we make it out to be.

Confidence is a perceived characteristic based on a set of observed behaviors. The perception of confidence can only be present when the breath is fully available in the body and the body is fully available to authentic expression, free of tension or resistance. These are the behaviors that we respond to when we perceive confidence. You see it in leaders; you see it in celebrities; you see it in people you admire. Maybe you desire to experience it for yourself, and that experience awaits you. It is already inside of you. It's just buried under a bunch of junk.

You cannot actually be confident. That may be an easy word to define your behavior or experience, but that is not what you are doing. You are not *doing* confidence. What you are doing is connecting to your breath, released in your body, expressive in your body and voice, with a distinct availability for play (that intangible space of unpredictability and aliveness). Those behavior habits will absolutely be perceived as confident. But confident is not what you are. It is not what you are seeking to become.

In the following chapters, I will guide you step by step in how to consider the notion of practice, how to focus the mind and habits in a way that makes this work accessible and sustainable for a lifetime of transformation, and all the skills you need to make you feel and appear as confident as you desire. I will give you all the tools. You must do the work. Let's get started.

LEARN

Unconscious Conditioning

For several years, I brought a program called "Plight of the Powerful Woman" around the world to various organizations and communities. My intention with the program was to facilitate collaborative discussions on what the future of female leadership looked like and what was required to get us there. The discussion always began with the simple question, "Where did we come from?" Specifically, the question challenges participants to identify the conditions that opened a culture to the notion of women as leaders within social and organizational systems.

I was hosting the program for a company in Amsterdam. The CEO was on the hot seat for some bad press around gender equity in senior leadership, and his solution was to bring women leaders of the organization together to see how the company could solve this problem and create more opportunity for women in leadership roles.

I started by having the room break into small groups to respond to the first question, "Where did we come from?" Observing small group discussions is fascinating. Watching body language escalate in sync with vocal tone. Watching people lean in and lean out depending on their adamance to argue their point. This group did not disappoint. From the start, they were deeply engaged. I think my favorite moments were observing genuine outbursts of laughter and the building of community in real time.

From the small groups, we came back together to do a collective harvest of ideas. One woman in her late fifties with wild hair, big gold earrings, and a bright green sweater offered that women were liberated through innovation. She cited such instances as how the rise of birth control allowed women to be empowered around their family planning and forgo the days of unwanted pregnancy. She said the advent of the microwave meant less time spent in the kitchen and more time pursuing education or employment. Another woman, earlier on in her leadership journey, offered a sociopolitical consequence based on her family history. She shared that wartime pulled the men in her family away from jobs that women were then asked to fill and ultimately hold, even after the war had ended.

There was energy and passion in the responses, almost like a vibrant brainstorm of subversive success. A recounting of our secret mission to rise from the shadows of society and emerge as essential parts of defining the future of social evolution. When I began with this group initially, I perceived apprehension and uncertainty, indicated through lack of eye contact, crossed arms and attention on devices rather than on the other women in the room.

What a difference a little truthful dialogue makes. I could see their imaginations being sparked and a gradual embracing of the permission to critically assess their position. They had been given the space to explore and identify their collective journey. I knew this group was going to determine some excellent solutions for the CEO.

We navigated through some seriously compelling discourse, finally making our way to the last question, "What is the future of female leadership?" and the answers were pretty unexpected. A junior-level woman, representing the voice of the next generation of leaders, blew everyone away when she said, "Gender will be irrelevant in another generation. The discussion on gender equity is necessary in the short term, but not for a long-term solution of diversity." This notion required a paradigm shift around the entire conversation of gender parity in leadership.

The comment that garnered the most consensus, however, was offered by a woman who had remained pretty reserved for most of the session. She mentioned she had been passed over for promotions on three different occasions, all of which were offered to men she had trained. It was almost too cliché to imagine until others in the room echoed her experience. Even in the face of what one could describe as blatant sexism, she promoted the following solution: "Women in leadership isn't the answer to equity. It's the quality of leadership that promotes equity and diversity in the long run."

This point really struck me. What the group uncovered was that in an attempt to address the gender equity challenge, the company had placed women on teams that were predominantly or historically composed only of men. The outcome was underperforming teams and dysfunctional workflows because the company mindset was on optics, not actual ability. Women were being placed in roles they were not a great fit for, reinforcing the notion that women are not suited for career advancement.

Besides women being moved laterally, few were being promoted. The organization favored leadership behavior devoid of sentiment or high emotional quotient. They were metric and money driven. This is a traditionally masculine approach to operating an organization, be it a publicly traded company or even government. The leadership qualities not celebrated were traditionally categorized as feminine.

The CEO had asked for action items toward creating gender parity and the only response he got was the group asking him simply why it mattered. See, the ultimate revelation from this particular program was that the women of the organization were not interested in gender parity or equity of female representation in leadership. What they really desired was an environment where feminine characteristics such as deep listening, compassion, patience, and creative thinking were celebrated and represented all the way through the executive level of leadership. Whether male or female leaders embodied those qualities or characteristics was irrelevant. It was the essence of the leadership that mattered most.

It would have been really easy to engage in this program half-heartedly, with total resignation to the status quo. Based on their initial apprehension, I was concerned these women would shy away from speaking their truth, having been conditioned to a system that had historically silenced them. But instead, through present and authentic dialogue, they were able to uncover a deeper need behind the challenge set forth by the CEO. They could have submitted a clean list of Band-Aid solutions, but they advocated for what they now knew to be true. They didn't offer solutions. They asked for deeper meaning.

So, how do you not only change a system, but change the humans *behind* the system?

How do you empower yourself to be a more empathetic CEO or a more outspoken employee? Start with understanding why you relegate yourself to what is familiar or safe, what are the unconscious beliefs that inform how you navigate your life, and how they are holding you hostage from speaking up and speaking your truth.

Here's the thing: Powerful systems are at play in your life that you have no control over or ability to change, but they contribute to your human suffering. They are historic, hereditary, and intricately pervasive. People of color, indigenous people, members of the LGBTQ community, women, and other historically disenfranchised groups operate within a system you can do very little individually to impact in a major way in order to make the system work for you. So much of what fuels these external conditions and circumstances is entirely outside of your control.

Building a practice of confidence is about empowering yourself to do what you can to feel you have the agency to engage in these systems, or any system you find yourself at odds with, and transform them from the inside out. You are in control of you and not much beyond that. It's not about changing the number of women in leadership; it's rather about developing the ability to say to a CEO of a Fortune 100 multinational organization, "Hey man, it's not enough to put women in leadership positions. It's about nurturing and advocating for the qualities of human behavior that result in well-being for me, my team, and the entire organization, so don't front with your disingenuous representation goals."

What the CEO does with that information is out of your control, but speaking up is up to you. Otherwise, you are choosing to simply resign yourself to live in the safe zone because you have established a belief that you are powerless to speak your truth or you consistently cater to the fear of consequence. We often make excuses why our suffering exists, and I know there is plenty of reason for suffering, but you have tremendous control over your attitude and your behavior. Placing your attention there instead of on the things you cannot change will transform your life.

Now you may think to yourself, "I didn't establish disempowering beliefs on purpose. I don't mean to let fear win. Why is this happening to me?" Rest assured—it's happening to all of us, in small ways, all the time. We are all subject to powerful social echo chambers with rigid narrative feedback loops that feel painfully inescapable. For example, we are being conditioned by algorithms as we speak. You know, the things that drive your Facebook feed or YouTube recommendations. You are being incrementally guided toward homogenous thought and reinforced belief systems from the tiny device you carry with you everywhere.

You get notifications from your news app sharing political updates and breaking news, but that news is never, well, *new*, is it? It's a repetitive narrative of crisis or breakthroughs in human rights that are quickly overshadowed by some new outcry of oppression, terror, or placating achievement. You are fed unrelenting disenfranchisement, and it takes tremendous fortitude to remove yourself from its grasp.

Even when you recognize that the news isn't helping your mental state, your internal belief systems can prevent you from becoming fully independent from your echo chamber. External systemic challenges and internal belief systems work in unison and often reinforce one another. You are equally complicit in reinforcing the systems at play. You may be caught up in an algorithm induced echo chamber, but the information that catalyzed that feedback loop resulted from manual input. Your input. And that input, whatever data you contributed to start the cycle, likely stems from opinions or areas of curiosity established very early that have been reinforced and embodied over the course of your life. This same example of algorithms and the notion of the echo chamber effect is clear in most social and political systems in which we find ourselves.

For the women in Amsterdam, they were staring inequity in the face, and they were the primary victims. Yet they stayed under the employment of that inequitable system and, up to the point of the powerful woman event, had done nothing to sincerely take action. They were feeling at odds with the system but remained embedded in the system. Why? I would urge you to consider where in your own life you are taking part in systems that don't match up with your values. What pressures have led you to participate?

This may be a conditioned understanding of your status in this world—being liked or disliked, feeling popular or unpopular, or perhaps your relationship to money and power—how you relate to those from different socioeconomic backgrounds or your drive to accumulate wealth or maybe live off the grid. It could look like a powerful presence of religion, as innocuous as a standard family association to a defined monotheistic belief system, such as Christianity. Or, as for a dear friend of mine, it could look like an adolescent conversion to a deeply religious community isolated from modern society, brought on by their father's personal crisis surrounding his own relationship to God, which my friend left only after succumbing to the pressures of conformity, including such events as very early marriage and multiple children.

We are being influenced by voices embedded in our psyches long ago and voices being reinforced in our present reality. We cannot presume immunity to these systems. Our conditioning takes place outside of our control. Until we decide to become conscious of these systems and take action by establishing new internal belief systems more aligned to our authentic values and that will ultimately shift our relationship to and behaviors around the more powerful systems at play, we will remain largely unconscious to this one life we are living.

For the women in Amsterdam, the primary system to examine was their relationship to patriarchal systems and how they had established unconscious beliefs around their capacity to operate with autonomy or empowerment to disrupt the system from within. This was likely conditioned in blatant ways through a consistently placed narrative of men as the archetype for leadership and in a more subtle way like when a mother says to her daughter when asked about why only men are leaders, the mother replies simply, "Don't worry about things like that."

You can stay asleep to these obstacles. You can choose to resign yourself to living a safe, conditioned life that is "fine" or "tolerable." Or you can come back to your body, sink into your breath, and find your voice for transformation. There is the choice to live safely or live confidently.

If you are feeling safe, but not alive, then are you really living?

If you are feeling like this is a daunting reality or have resigned to the impossibility of living authentically within such a monolithic system, I want to assure you that you are capable of remarkable things and unlocking your full potential is a noble devotion of your time and energy during this one life you are conscious to.

In fact, when you're on your deathbed, isn't that what will matter most? Bronnie Ware, best known for her book *The Top Five Regrets of the Dying*, was interviewed in *Forbes* and when asked what she assessed to be the most painful regret she had witnessed in the dying, she shared, "Wishing you'd live a life true to yourself, not the life other people expected of you. Whether those other people are family, peers, or society makes no difference. The utter heartache of dying with that regret, because you didn't bring enough courage to the choices you made, is a painful way to end your life." (Caprino, 2019) Let that image sink in, and experience that sense of regret. Not taking risks on love, never standing up for what's right, or dismissing the desire to pursue a passion that others deemed frivolous.

What is it all for, if not to experiment with the gift of your unique life, free from constraint of expectation or unconscious conditioning?

You entered this world with the complete power to share your authentic voice. If you were hungry, you spoke up. If you were tired, you cried until someone put you down for a nap. You never had a sense that you needed your diaper changed but saw that your mom was busy and you didn't want to bother her, so you just sat in a soiled diaper until it felt okay to interrupt. Heck no! You began your life in full empowerment. You could cry for hours and not lose your voice. Your little body was free of tension and could move in naturally expressive, unencumbered ways. You had no problem asking for what you needed and demanding what you wanted.

But somewhere along the line, through a series of incremental and unconscious shifts, your desire for a safe life superseded your desire for living. All of a sudden, this innate experience and behavior of empowerment became degraded and buried under ego, expectation, caution, and fear. You lost your sense of play and wonder.

Perhaps your everlasting voice became narrow, constrained, tense, or lost the stamina for advocating for its inner child.

Perhaps your perfect posture became hunched from shrinking against your circumstance or tight from overcompensating against a fear of not being seen or liked or appreciated.

Perhaps your ability to speak your truth and advocate for your needs became a distant memory in the face of never feeling like those needs were met, so you stopped bothering to express them.

Patsy Rodenburg, in her book *The Right to Speak,* reflects on this process, saying, "Gradually these habits, which we take to be natural, enslave us. We become restricted in what we can say and how we say it." What she's referring to are the habits we create to keep us safe that eventually become our default behavior. We learn to not speak up or shrink ourselves to not be seen. This becomes familiar and we define it as our natural state.

I had a client who was extremely accomplished. She is a senior leader for a large company, leading the success of multiple business units. She is quite tall, outspoken, and very smart. But she harbored tremendous resentment around not being accepted and developed habits to protect herself. She grew up in a small southern town where she felt out of place. Her politics didn't align with her community. She felt as a woman that she had to force her way into being seen. She was consistently rejected in her vision and value and developed the habit of speaking in a dominating, loud voice, almost with an attitude of, "I know you don't want to hear me, but I'm going to force you to listen."

I was called in by her boss to support her to get her ideas heard. It was identified that although she had tremendous vision, her approach to communicating that vision was creating a defense response from the executive team. At the start of our work together, she expressed experiencing consistent vocal strain. She felt like she lost her train of thought more regularly than she liked. She was also aware that her relationship to the "patriarchy" was troubled and was a strong contributor to her habits, at work and in her personal life. She is married to a man, has a validation-based relationship to her father, and her executive team at work consisted of older white men.

These were her circumstances. She was a fighter. She thought she had to be. All of those circumstances were beyond her control. My job was to address what was within her control. Throughout the course of our work, I encouraged her to keep her fight, retain her passion, but implement three new behavior habits:

1. slow down her speech → challenging her to gain presence around how her thoughts were leaving her mouth

2. consciously observe her breath in her belly → which grounded her energy and enabled deeper listening

3. soften the muscles in her forehead before she opened her mouth to speak → which promotes warmer tones in her voice and less forceful vocalization

The important thing I want to call your attention to here is that none of what we worked on dealt with resolving her past trauma. It was not about justifying her experience or behavior based on the suffering she experienced through her circumstance. Like the women in Amsterdam, we didn't resolve her relationship to the patriarchy. What we addressed was the behavior and physical habits she had developed to keep herself safe as a child and throughout her developmental years that had since become natural to her but were ultimately undermining her desire to be seen, heard, and celebrated. We broke it down to facts.

By focusing on what was within her control, she now had actionable goals to transform her life, feel connected to her desires, and express herself authentically, rather than relying on the habits that held her hostage. She could shift into behaviors of confidence and escape the shackles of arrogance.

Arrogance, along with confidence, is a perception. If confidence is breath fully available in the body and a body fully available to expression, then arrogance is its foil. Arrogance is perceived when tension is present, when the breath is tight and held in the chest, when the expression of the body feels fueled by anxiety, and communication seems erratic or forceful in nature. It can be confused with confidence until you soften your gaze and realize that confidence can be received by the listener. Arrogance may only be observed. One is for connecting. One is for protecting.

After our work together and her consistent attention to functional communication techniques for the months following our engagement, she was promoted and given the green light on a powerful diversity initiative she had been developing for quite some time. This outcome was not because she changed her circumstances and upset the system that was holding her back. She stepped out of her safety zone and took charge of what was within her control, shifting her behavior, and changed her relationship to the system from the inside out.

I have seen this transformation time and time again. Clients come to me desiring deeper connection to their life. They have come to a place in their journey where they know there is untapped potential but cannot seem to access it or even know what it is they are looking for. Can you relate to this feeling? This feeling like you suddenly wake up one day and the routine that has enslaved you for years almost instantaneously becomes unbearable. You see your career and know there has to be more. You witness your relationships and feel a sincere yearning for greater depth. You observe yourself consciously, maybe for the first time, and see someone walking through life safely, but not truly alive.

It is in these moments when we begin the search for answers or archetypes. You see people within your community that embody the life you want for yourself. You see people around you effortlessly make friends, get promotions, fall in love, and analyze how they do it. You read books on becoming a better version of yourself. You research manifestation and become the newest member of Oprah's book club. You awaken yourself to the notion of "abundance" and "high vibration." And then what? You have filled yourself with intellectual knowledge of how to lead the life you want, outside of your safety zone, but how do you put all of that into practice?

How do you become the most alive version of yourself and start living the life you want?

You must start by understanding what it is you are truly seeking to explore, and odds are, it has a lot to do with confidence. As you move out of your safe life and dip your toe into the pool of confidence, it is necessary to define what confidence is. Confidence is not a thing you are; it is a thing that is experienced by others. It is a perceived characteristic based on a set of behaviors that gives the impression of confidence. Along with this definition, we must understand that how we are perceived and how others identify and contextualize confidence is entirely beyond our control. However, I will encourage you that no matter how others perceive you, if you are activating fully authentic behaviors, you will be perceived as a confident person, however that manifests. Strong voice, subtle voice, broad gesture, simple movement. There is no defining image.

When you are fully yourself, in the presence of truth, who you are is just perfect.

The behaviors you are looking to authentically cultivate are few but mighty. Confidence can only be perceived when the breath is fully available in the body and the body is fully available to expression, without anticipation, tension, or predetermination. Confidence is not a mindset or an attitude. You do not fake it until you make it. You are not layering on a cloak of a future you hoping that it will eventually fit.

Instead, you are peeling away the layers of those "natural" habits and becoming more deeply yourself. Doing less to allow for more. You are not seeking confidence. You are seeking authenticity and presence. Three things will guide you into that experience: open body, open breath, and freedom of voice. If those three elements are authentically present and behaviors of those three elements are authentic to you in their expression, confidence will be perceived. The pursuit of confidence is a fool's errand. The pursuit of authenticity is a noble adventure. The confident body is one that is free to be unapologetically true to itself. If your body is speaking its truth, I guarantee the world will listen.

What I love about this definition is that it puts the power of confidence in anyone's hands because it implies that the behaviors of confidence can be learned, developed, and amplified. It democratizes confidence rather than having it be an aspirational quality reserved for the lucky few born with a predisposition for greatness. It unifies rather than divides. It is no longer a matter of haves versus have nots.

We are all capable of living in a confident body.

Observation

What would you like to do with your body that you don't currently do? For example, you really want to have the courage to speak up in meetings, but consistently stop yourself. What is the experience of negating that impulse? Perhaps you experience a physical sensation of restlessness or distraction in the shoulders or chest, often outcomes of fear, anxiety, dread, or an impulse gone unexpressed. It's like a sneeze you hold in or an answer you keep to yourself.

How does negating this impulse impact your breath? Where do you feel it exists in the body? Bring awareness to that area and resist the urge to fidget or fix. Notice the tension between wanting to fix and trying not to fix. The tension between knowing what to notice in the body and waiting for the thing to be noticed to reveal itself. Notice the tension in the moment of reading this direction and the body's response to reading new information. Are you breathing right now?

Observing the body during its function in everyday tasks, its response to everyday experiences, and how it operates when all by itself is likely not something you have consciously done before. You may be very aware that you stop yourself from speaking up in meetings and wish you could magically find the courage to do so, but have you thought about how your body prepares to meet the impulse to speak up? Does your body retreat or advance? Does your jaw tighten? Do you hold your breath in your chest? Does your voice get caught in the throat and feel blocked in the process of release?

We spend a tremendous amount of time considering how we come across or what others think about us. We get lost in the question of why we can't do the things we want to do or behave the way we want to behave. We want to speak up in the meeting and think that there is something wrong with us for not being able to "just do it." We operate in a land of trying to do something without actually taking the time to break down the steps of the actual doing versus the aspirational doing.

You are encouraged to just "be confident" without taking the time to identify what needs to functionally shift for you in order to step into your authenticity. This approach leads to a destructive cycle of desire to act, denial of action, and judgment of inaction. It is easy to become discouraged or reinforce the belief that confidence just isn't available to you. What if, instead, you approached the situation with an observant lens and built a plan for behavior change based on the data you collect—the facts versus the feelings?

For example: I know that when I walk into a meeting, my body tends to tense up when I see the other people present and I get small in my shoulders. I feel my gaze lower, and I have a strong sensation in my chest telling me to avoid eye contact. When I sit down, my spine is collapsed, and my hips are tight. I am taking shallow breaths. My focus is on hoping I can speak up today instead of listening deeply in order to respond effortlessly to the conversation taking place.

Observation is the most powerful tool for transformation. We cannot change what we cannot see.

If you experience a lack of confidence in some area of your life, nothing will come from simply willing more confidence. That means nothing from a functional perspective, although it may be reassuring in the short term. The key is to objectively gather information about how you physically resist or allow your body to operate within confident behaviors, in various circumstances, where you feel out of alignment with your authenticity, i.e., speaking in public, meeting new people, or setting clear boundaries.

Objective observation of self allows you to gather information around your connection to breathe, openness in body, freedom in voice, and availability to play. You must distance your observation from your opinion about yourself. The information you gather is not good, bad, or indifferent. It has nothing to do with your intrinsic value. It is simply an identification of physical behavior habits that are not allowing you to operate at your fullest potential.

Having an objective and functional lens as you observe and redirect your behavior habits is paramount to success in this process. Beware the judging mind. It will creep in. You will have challenging opinions about yourself and the process.

Receive that as information, likely a reflection of a deeper fear or area of vulnerability. That is where the magic happens.

Although we are not seeking a defined outcome of this work in terms of how confidence will come alive in you, we can view success as a process that feels affirmative, easy, and enlivening. Let that be your North Star. As you initiate your practice of observation, take a moment to consider your mindset going into the work. Are you entering into the work with urgency? With a desire to fix or solve a problem?

Let me remind you that you are not broken. You are not in need of fixing.

Carrying a sense of urgency or obligation will undermine sincere attempts at transformation. Think about it like starting a diet or exercise routine. You might start a routine that is motivated by a historic pattern of negative self-talk. You may call yourself fat or gross (that was my word) and convince yourself that you must lose weight to be attractive. But by doing that, exercising becomes a punishment or a chore. You feel obligated to exercise rather than inspired to exercise. Not only that, but you are also working toward an external transformation based on aesthetic rather than an internal transformation based on vitality, form, and function. Always be in service of the potential of your body, not the perfection of your body.

This shift in narrative and intention allows you to engage with a lens of possibility rather than punishment and will encourage a sustainable level of focus during the process of developing behaviors of confidence. I encourage you to establish a possibility mindset that will serve as your anchor as you initiate the practices. It is easier than you think to forget why you're doing what you're doing and, as a result, lose presence in the doing itself.

Even people who have the best intentions of presence and purpose are prone to falter.

In my group coaching course, where we study the practices and principles outlined in this book, all of the participants are high performers and established experts. They enroll in my course with a clear purpose and desire for transformation. It is a distinctly intentional space. I begin every cohort by teaching a voice and body practice that they will revisit throughout the course. I ask that everyone submit a video of their practice between classes so I can offer feedback on form and function within the movements.

The practice is a modified version of a longer practice developed by Chuck Jones. It is a series of exercises centered around the spine and release of breath in accordance with movement. For example, after we have gone through a full-body check-in, I direct them to plant their focus on the breath and the skeleton. They are in a standing position, so the goal is effortless activation. The first movement is to drop the chin toward the chest on the exhale, followed by slowly rolling down through the spine.

There are several moments to observe as the practitioner—the moment before you begin, the moment you exhale and release the chin to chest, the act of initiating rolling down through your spine, the adjustment of your feet as your center of balance shifts, etc.

Inevitably, the videos I receive after the first class, their very first opportunity to practice observing how they engage in the work, predictably lack a clear intentionality in the movement and do not demonstrate conscious observation. What I observe are a series of videos, all displaying various parts of the practice, that are perfunctory in the execution. They are doing the practices for homework, not as a process of authentic inquiry. This default behavior in how they practice is a habit in and of itself—mindless over mindful. And this is not for lack of trying. I see them in the videos wanting to "get it." To do well and excel. I see shallow breathing "deep inhales" followed by an immediate shift into a roll down, completely skipping over the chin drop, an expedited rolling down of the spine, and a mindless restacking of the vertebrae as they make their way back to standing. This is not a judgment. It is a factual observation. The person might be nervous about filming themselves, or not used to fully engaging with their body, or even self-conscious about taking the assignment seriously. Regardless of the motivation, the behaviors exist.

This tells me they are not conscious of the movement, much less how the breath is operating within the movement. They did not create intentional space for observing the body as it interacts and experiences the practice. I guarantee this was not their intention, to deliver videos devoid of presence.

Pro tip: The slower you go, the faster you get there.

This will allow conscious movement versus mindless movement. Mindless practice can lead to a reinforcement of old habits rather than an activation of presence and redirection into new habits. So again, I will encourage you to consider wisely how you are entering into this work: obligation or opportunity?

There is a foundational premise to the work of conscious redirection found in the Alexander Technique, a human performance method designed to support optimal physical use during public speaking and stage acting, that is, "how you do anything is how you do everything." This means that how you show up in a challenging conversation is likely echoed in how you interact with someone at the supermarket and even down to how you engage in a nighttime routine. Your habits and mannerisms are pervasive, especially where the voice and muscles of communication are concerned. The challenge, of course, is that you are likely not conscious to your momentary behavior of how you do anything, much less everything. That is what we will uncover here:

HOW TO INITIATE BUILDING A HABIT OF OBSERVATION OF USE

The first step is remembering to observe an action or behavior. I spent an hour going over the practice with my group coaching students. I broke down the key moments for observation, and they still skipped the steps. Behavior change starts with remembering that you intend to change your behavior.

The mind is a tricky monster.

You can start with an innocuous activity, such as washing the dishes. You can begin the practice simply by acknowledging consciously that you are washing dishes. I am aware how insignificant that sounds, but I would venture to guess that you have a tendency to do the dishes start to finish without ever acknowledging during the process that you are, in fact, doing the dishes. That your hands are wet or observing how you reach for the sponge or bend down to open the dishwasher. To register how your breath is present during the action or how your jaw is tight or released depending on the quantity of dishes to tackle.

The important thing is to process all the data as a statement of fact, not feeling.

After you build the habit of acknowledging when an action is taking place, you can then break down the macro action into micro actions. In the example of washing dishes, the macro action is washing dishes. The micro actions are leaning forward to turn on the faucet, the pressure with which you squeeze water from the sponge, the way your feet are making contact with the kitchen floor. You become the observer of your own actions as well as the primary participant and executor of the actions.

You must be both self-aware and unattached to the outcome of that awareness.

This is where objectivity is vital. Feedback, even for yourself, is not about you as a person. It is about the action or behavior that resulted in a specific outcome, desired or undesired. Period. When you wash the dishes and notice that you are squeezing the sponge with incredible force, instead of making judgment about why that is or what reflection that has on your intrinsic value as a person, start by asking yourself if that form of use or habit is requiring more or less effort than is needed. Does the sponge need to be squeezed that hard and how does the rest of the body compensate in response to such a forceful squeeze? Does the core over-engage and maybe you tighten your lower back? Does your butt tense up and thrust your pelvis forward? Do you lose connection to easy breathing?

We are a series of actions and reactions. Nothing happens without something else happening in response.

Week one, choose one daily activity you perform with regularity and commit to consciously registering how you engage in that activity over the course of one week. This may be driving to work, walking to the subway, or flossing your teeth. Choose the activity and do what is required to be accountable to observation. As we have acknowledged previously, it is remarkably easy to forget our best intentions. Write it on a Post-it note, set a reminder in your phone, etc. Make it obvious and easy. Once you have selected the activity, each day simply begin by registering that you are engaged in the activity. "I am driving." "I am flossing my teeth." This will build the practice of observation as well as cultivate easy habits of presence within that activity.

Week two, continue with the observation of your daily activity and add an additional layer to the exercise by observing your physical use within that activity. You can begin by identifying the micro actions within the macro action, but I will encourage you to think about the use versus the action or task. Easy points of use to observe are 1) level of access to easy breath, 2) tension or activation of shoulder muscles, and 3) the knees. When you are flossing your teeth, are you breathing? Are your shoulders tense or lifted as you reach your back molars? Are your knees locked or hyper-extended? This process of observation is one of curiosity. I am certain you haven't spent dedicated time assessing the use of your body in such mundane tasks. How you do anything is how you do everything. These macro actions or activities are solitary in nature. This is important.

We must first observe ourselves free from our relational habits with others.

Once you have spent a couple of weeks observing yourself in solitude, repeat the same process in a shared activity. Maybe this is a carpool or a team meeting. Week one, consciously register yourself participating in the interaction or relationship: "I am at the meeting." And follow that with a week of observing your use as you engage in that interaction or relationship: "My gaze is directed down for the majority of the meeting, and I feel my jaw tense up as my neck becomes fatigued." We are focusing on your behavior. We are not focusing on who is in the room that caused your gaze to direct downward. That is outside of our control and focused on feeling over fact.

Stay observant of what is within your control, which is your breath, body, and objectivity with which you define your circumstances.

The final layer of daily observation will happen after you observe your physical use in relationship. This layer is observing the experience of the voice. It is very typical to shift vocal tone and quality depending on who you are interacting with, your history with that person, or your status or power dynamic with that person. We call this vocal masking. For example, you may be a leader within an organization and have developed vocal habits, along with physical habits, around how you communicate with your team. Those habits are likely quite different from how you would speak to your mother or romantic partner.

Beyond the language, consider pitch, presence and freedom of vibration, and overall availability of vocal dynamics and tonal fluctuation. When you speak to your team, you may be very direct in your tone. Perhaps you experience the vibration centered around the chest and coming from the belly. Then your mother calls right in the middle of a meeting. You answer the phone and, without even realizing it, your tone has moved up in pitch and your experience of vibration is centered around the mask area or right between the eyes. Your voice is really vibration. It can be distinctly felt and will have a variety of pitches depending on the frequency and wavelength of the vibration as it travels through and ultimately exits the body. This is not good, bad, or indifferent. It is simply a fact.

If you really struggle to observe yourself objectively at first, you can begin by observing others.

This can serve as a powerful calibration tool. It is important to resist comparison or judgment in this process. Even when we are observing others, we are focused on facts, not feelings.

What do you notice in regard to their posture? Do you have an awareness of where they hold tension or limit their breathing? Does their voice shift when they interact with different people? Do you have an easy or hard time listening to or connecting with them? Perhaps they are loud, focused on volume versus vibration. Maybe they are forceful in simple actions, like opening a beer bottle. Notice what you notice. Then turn the lens on yourself.

In the process of observation, you will collect a wealth of information. You do not need to know what to do with it yet. You are consciously observing at this stage, not redirecting what you observe. Not yet. Begin with building the practice and habit of observation. It's not terribly exciting in terms of momentum and visible progress, but it will lay a foundation for much deeper and lasting behavior change as the process continues.

Now You See It

When I was a kid, there was a fad sweeping the nation called *Magic Eye* 3D illusions. It was a book series where there were kaleidoscope-like images on a page, repeated pictures of buildings or of flowers, and if you stared at it long enough and in just the right way, an image would appear among the patterns. This image had a 3D quality, seeming to jump off the page. I was obsessed with these things. How something that appeared to be one thing, transformed into this secret something else. Once I finally saw the 3D image of any given page, that now became the reality. Once I saw it, I couldn't unsee it.

The conditions of your safe life are like *Magic Eye*. Once you bring your unconscious beliefs and behaviors into focus, you can't unsee them. The system in which you live is designed to keep you from seeing in three dimensions. It takes conscious observation to see something beyond the established landscape.

We are conditioned from the very beginning, with no deliberate intention to arrest our potential, but rather as a consequence of generations of compliance, to fall in line and walk the narrow path established and maintained by those who came before and for those who will come after. These systems exist for a reason. They are a proven system of survival over many generations, and our compliance to the system is engrained at every angle. The challenge is when these systems no longer serve us, but we are unable to break free or even see where they are suppressing the expression of our authentic self.

Your two-dimensional life shows up in all aspects. You have likely experienced it in your nuclear household. Maybe your mom stayed home while dad went to work to earn enough to "keep a roof over your head" and "put food on the table," so you grew up with the conditioned understanding that traditionally women stayed home while men went out to provide and this was the "right way" to build a future. Maybe you grew up with only one parent who assumed both the caretaker and provider roles but wasn't home all that much because they were working two jobs to make ends meet. This gave you freedom to devote a lot of time to your friend group, who became your primary moral compass. Maybe they made choices aligned to your values. Maybe they didn't. But eventually you assumed their behavior because it was safe, familiar, and reliable.

These conditions and behaviors are all driven through deeply ingrained belief systems that started well before we came into being. They are passed down from generation to generation, iterated upon, and reinforced. They may present themselves in ways such as an expectation to pursue a lucrative career because financial stability is a priority over emotional or creative fulfillment. Perhaps the belief is that life will always be a struggle and the chances of escaping the struggle of financial hardship are impossible, so expectations of success or achievement are very low.

In his acclaimed work, *The Body Keeps the Score: Brain, Mind, and Body in the Healing of Trauma,* Bessel van der Kolk, MD, illuminates such patterns, as reflected on the individual, through his research on early childhood trauma and its impact on emotional and psychological development into adulthood. He offers, "If a mother cannot meet her baby's impulses and needs, 'the baby learns to become the mother's idea of what the baby is.' Having to discount its inner sensations and trying to adjust to its caregiver's needs means the child perceives there is 'something wrong' with the way it is." In this example, this baby is conditioned early on to dismiss the signals of the essential and authentic expression of self and defer to the patterns that will best serve safety and maintenance of relationship to the primary caregiver. In this case, becoming what they should be rather than who they are. This is just one example of how systems in which we did not make conscious decisions to participate affect the evolution of self *away* from self.

These conditions and belief systems impact the way in which you develop physical habits around communication, relationships, and the pursuit of goals. If you are nurtured toward excellence, perhaps you develop habits of perfectionism— manifest through tension—and avoid the outcome of failure at all costs, even if that means losing grains of humanity or authenticity. You'd rather be right than be real. Maybe you were lacking consistent emotional support, so you develop habits of coping through repressing and dismissing your feelings. You'd rather be fine than alive.

These habits are carried with you. They become "natural" and keep you safe. The expected path transforms from an external framework to an internal belief system. It is not until we question it, that we see beyond its boundary. In the meantime, existing within a rigid system can dramatically impact our development and personal evolution. We become trapped in the adaptive behavior habits of our bodies and neglect the process of finding our way to authentic embodiment of the truest version of ourselves.

At the time I was in graduate school, at the age of twenty-four, I found myself deeply entrenched in unconscious and conditioned beliefs. I was existing within a cultural belief system of a linear path for how my life should evolve (college, graduate school, marriage, professional success, money, death).

I was engaged to a lovely man from New Hampshire, who was a sound engineer. We met on Myspace (go ahead and have a chuckle at that one) and had been dating since I was nineteen. I had not been in many relationships—okay, any relationships—prior to him. I had no understanding of what it felt like to be in love, although I had had my fair share of crushes. So, when we got together and eventually fell in love, I thought I had met a milestone. I am aware of the unromantic description in that, but it was true. I felt quite superior that at the supple age of nineteen I had already found "the one." I was playing the part of a dutiful daughter, walking my path toward death.

Where I came from in Appalachia, it was not uncommon to get married very young. I saw this play out for so many of the women I went to school with, many of whom had at least one child by the time I was entering graduate school. In addition, my parents, although liberal and advocates for independence, also ingrained a traditional path into how we should envision our lives.

By the time I was entering graduate school, I had been with my soon-to-be husband for four years. We fought a lot. I was constantly disappointed in him. He was constantly frustrated with me. We were operating from very different unconscious belief systems, and this led to tremendous conflict. But one of the other narratives that was reinforced by so many, was that relationships are supposed to be hard, especially at the beginning. So, I stuck with it, in spite of the turmoil and resentment—although I was finding myself attracted to other men and had almost no sexual relationship with my future husband. I stuck with it.

Along with my arrogance of linear achievement, came a stubborn commitment to following through. This required a silencing of my intuition and an amplification of feigned satisfaction. I remember meeting my husband at the altar and bursting into tears. I convinced myself it was because I was so happy, but I know now it was because I knew I was making a terrible mistake and was feeling so ashamed. My body released its truth despite my best effort to keep it quiet.

I remember two years later when, after having disappeared for three days, my husband came home, sat next to me, and told me he was not in love with me and wasn't sure if he ever had been. I was devastated, still operating in a belief system of "for better or for worse." Two months later, after I had moved out, I finally saw it. I was not in love with him either. I had been blindly walking the expected path, and now I was being given the tremendous gift of deviation. I saw it and couldn't unsee it.

One year later, I was divorced, and that was the greatest outcome possible. Not because he was bad, or I was bad. We were simply walking different paths. My body felt lighter and alive. I felt like I was witnessing life in an entirely new way.

I have such gratitude for my ex-husband for having the courage to step outside of his safe life and risk demolishing what was familiar and established. He gave me such a gift in that. He opened my eyes to the safe life I was living. We are no longer married, but I have to credit my ex-husband for setting me on a path toward becoming the person I am today.

I urge you to reflect on where you feel at odds with your life, the system in which you exist.

This experience of friction may manifest as a consistent experience of dread around a relationship or a feeling of resentment around your work. It may present itself in daydreams or in your quiet moments where the brain softens just enough to finally speak the truth of your subconscious.

You are reading this book because you feel like there is something more for you. You have untapped potential. Honor that wisdom and amplify its voice. This is your time to establish a new path. I encourage you to start taking notes. Notice what excites you, what motivates you, versus what makes you feel small, invisible, or full of dread, and write it down.

The joy of this work is in the unremarkable moments of discovery. If you try to rush the process, you will miss the process entirely or risk the process never actually taking hold. The joy comes in those moments when, without even realizing it, you make a choice that differs from your historical habits. You start to see, in small ways, your full potential emerges.

What is within your control is this moment. What is not within your control is the exact shape your full potential takes.

Let yourself be in awe of yourself and surprise yourself with your transformation. Stay open to not knowing. If you are constantly forcing a predetermined outcome, attached to a narrow vision of what you will accept as the end result, then you are simply building different habits to keep you safe.

Remember, we are all capable of living in a confident body. What that body looks like is the mysterious treasure you will discover along the way and what is found within the process itself. Stay present, stay curious, stay open to adaptation and transformation.

I am named after my grandmother, Minna (she went by Min). She was an incredible woman. Her mother died shortly after giving birth to her. Her father didn't know what to do with a little girl as a single father. This was back in 1917, so he sent her to live with her aunts. They were immigrants from Bavaria. My grandmother was born into a world of unexpected outcomes and nonideal circumstances. Yet she managed to take action where she could and that ultimately led her to become a mother to two doctors and the first woman real estate agent in South Carolina to enter the million-dollar sales club.

Min lived to be 102 years old. Toward the end of her life, I asked her what she thought was the key to her longevity. In a very lucid tone, without skipping a beat, she said, "Adaptability." She was reflecting on all that had happened in her life and where she ended up, in a beautiful retirement community just outside of Charleston, South Carolina, to her extraordinary ability to adapt to her circumstances. She never resigned. She persevered. She stayed present, curious, and open. I carry this with me every day.

In approaching systems and circumstances, in beginning the journey to uncover and shift old habits, in pursuing a process that is largely unknown, you must embrace adaptability.

You have to maintain simple curiosity and have tremendous patience with yourself and those around you. As you move through your confidence journey, it comes down to you making a decision to do the work, and hopefully experiencing a little joy along the way. That is all you can control.

Status and Power

As a reward for being here, I offer you a diary entry:

> *Me: "Your reaction to my apparent mistake was so strongly negative and full of frustration that it made me really upset, self-conscious, embarrassed, and not sure if I wanted to continue."*

> *Professor: "Your response caused you to throw the baby out with the bath water. I only ask you to consider your response—whether you agree or disagree with the particulars is ultimately not nearly as important as the fact that you felt you abandoned your work as a result."*

This particular diary entry was from my graduate school improv class and, despite what may be fair to assume based on the above interaction, I really loved this class.

Improv is an extraordinarily important practice. It's not about being funny, a common misconception, but rather about absolute willingness to surrender, commit, and tell the truth. The most adept improvisers are the ones most willing to embrace vulnerability. It takes courage to fully commit to telling the truth in pursuit of an essential need and welcome the likelihood of looking foolish along the way.

There's a great analogy in the theater used to describe the difference between comedy and drama, which is that in drama, when you hear an unexpected knock at the door, you slowly rise and walk around the couch to open the door. In comedy, when an unexpected knock is at the door, you jump over the couch to answer the door. The stakes are higher in comedy, even in low-stakes scenarios. That's why we love sitcoms. It's regular people acting in extraordinary ways over situations that are largely immaterial (insert *Seinfeld* reference here).

This diary entry from improv class was in reference to an exercise called *Private Life*. At some point in the semester, we were all assigned a class where we would be the central character. The goal of the exercise is to explore vulnerability and depth of experience through the power of long form improvised role play. The central character stands alone in the center of the room. At any moment, a member of the class will enter their space and assume a character from their life, i.e., mother, younger sister, first love, etc. They then proceed to improvise a moment in time from that relationship based on the specific details offered by the person entering the space, i.e., what age would the central character be, what is their general attitude about life, what is the central conflict occurring at that moment and why.

In order to keep building the life of the central character, at any moment, another member of the class could clap, call freeze, and replace the current role play with a new scenario and new character in the central character's life. This rotation would last for about thirty minutes and then we would reflect on the experience as a group.

On this particular day, during a *Private Life* session, I clapped, signaling I would freeze the current scene and intended to step in as a new character, when my teacher abruptly shut me down. I was caught off guard, embarrassed, and furious. Even in reading her notes, all these years later, I have such a deep visceral memory of the moment. I can't tell you who was the central character or what the scene was even about, but I can tell you that humiliation persists in the body, and when I read her notes, over ten years later, I cried.

It's remarkable how these moments stay with us. As I'm reviewing her notes and reflecting on my experience, I am thinking about how embarrassed I was at being shut down and the way it challenged my vulnerability. But also, in my current state, how regretful I feel about such a missed opportunity for learning. I feel equally indignant to her behavior and in advocacy of her behavior. She gave me a valuable gift in what she communicated in her notes, but I was not available to receive it. When she says that I "abandoned my work as a result," she was absolutely right. She was a professor in a high-status position enforcing a wise perspective, but my vulnerable ego and resistance to authority prevented me from being a willing recipient of her wisdom. We are constantly being influenced or impacted by status and power while simultaneously seeking to possess status and power.

The negotiation of power dynamics and shifting status roles is at the heart of human relationships. How you allow this negotiation to unfold is at the center of living a confident life.

This plays out very concretely in the theater: the audience and the actor. The actor has high status by way of focal point, being the center of attention, and having primary control over how the performance will unfold. The audience has lower status by being positioned apart from and potentially below the actor; they are (usually) not encouraged to speak or actively contribute to the unfolding of the performance, and they are subject to whatever the performance is—good, bad, or indifferent. This is the status quo.

The exciting thing, and often the most unnerving, risky, or ego-confronting, is that status can change at any moment. The actor forgets their lines or makes an improvised joke that falls flat and all of a sudden, the actor's status drops as the audience loses confidence in them as a performer. The actor is now at the mercy of the audience to re-engage their attention and connection to the performance taking place. Like actors and audience, we are in constant negotiation of status and power dynamics. We must remain present to the shift, stay curious and observant, and learn how to respond rather than deny or overreact.

In the moment of *Private Life*, when I was cut off, how could I have resisted the urge to retreat into the comfort and safety of my righteous ego instead of shutting down? How could I have held my status and maintained my power while simultaneously respecting the status of my professor and surrendering to her power without fear of losing my power in the process?

Improv is all about "yes, and." The ability to acknowledge, elevate, and advance. It requires deep listening, collaboration, and creative problem solving. Unfortunately, we are socially conditioned toward the habit of "no, but," which results in dismissal, stagnation, and erosion of relationship. It takes vulnerability to live a "yes, and" life, the willingness to surrender, defer status, and receive someone else's power by relinquishing full control. During the *Private Life* exercise and in so many other instances during graduate school, I was in conflict with a desire to play in the space of "yes, and" and my willingness to release the safety of my "no, but" behavior.

I was watching a TEDx Talk with Keith Johnstone, the father of modern improvisation, called "Don't Do Your Best" where he offers, "Those who say 'yes' are rewarded by the adventures they have. Those who say 'no' are rewarded by the safety they attain." In this period of my life, I was attached to the safety of my controlled relationship to status and power. The adventure began when I learned to say 'yes,' which transformed how I behaved in relationship to status, power, and my conditioned understanding of what was possible for my life ahead.

Graduate school was a real turning point for me. I was coming from an elite undergraduate institution, a school that was the top school for acting in the country and entering a graduate training program with nine other students lacking the depth of training I had received. I had already categorized myself as a higher status performer.

I knew the curriculum would be a continuation of the fundamental techniques I had learned in undergrad; specifically, speech and phonetics, the voice technique outlined by Chuck Jones, and the acting technique called Practical Aesthetics. I was genuinely excited to deepen my exploration of these methodologies until I realized that we were starting from square one. I would not be continuing. I would be starting over.

You know the feeling when someone is telling you about something they think is really interesting, but you already know about it, so you're not really paying attention and instead thinking, *Yeah, yeah, yeah, I know this already*, and impatiently waiting for them to stop talking so you can move onto a new topic? That was my experience during my first year in grad school.

I had learned the techniques once already, and in my underdeveloped mind, I assumed that meant I knew it all. I carried this holier than thou attitude and secret assumption of superiority over my classmates. I would be paired with someone for a scene study and immediately create expectations of how "good" or "bad" they would be to work with and whether they could step up to my level.

Even as I write this thought, I cringe at my arrogance, but it's reality. I would sit in class, listening to my professors give feedback to my classmates, roll my eyes at how obvious it all was, and sink into my frustration that we weren't being challenged to go deeper. My voice and speech classes became afterthoughts because I thought I already knew it all. I had been teaching it already for nearly a year, after all. Of course, now I understood I had learned it intellectually, but was far from a sincere embodiment of the practices and principles. Coming back to basics for the first year as a review was honestly a tremendous opportunity that I squandered out of arrogant dismissal.

Along with the fog of my inflated ego, came my need to be validated and approved of by those whom I perceived held the power. Growing up, I felt love was conditional on performance. Get good grades, get a dollar and a hug. Say the right thing in public, get a pat on the back. Say the wrong thing in public, get sent to the car and forced to stay there because you were not fit for the world outside. Do good, get rewarded. Do bad, get punished.

I had developed the "natural" habit of seeking approval from authority figures in order to determine my value.

This resulted in a conflicted pursuit of my work, where on the one hand I was arrogant in my knowledge of certain techniques and on the other hand I was insecure and in need of acceptance and approval in the execution of those techniques. I would rehearse a scene with a classmate and subtly control the entire process, assuming I knew best. I would direct my fellow actor toward my superior vision for how the scene should go. Then we would get into class and present the scene, and I would desperately want my teacher to sing my praises and confirm my presumed ability. I was confident in my capability as an actress, but I needed that confidence to be explicitly affirmed in order for it to be true or valid. It's like being in a romantic relationship and only trusting your partner loves you if they tell you all the time rather than trusting that the love exists without condition, constant reinforcement, or expectation.

In this self-conscious, validation-based relationship pattern, love can never truly exist because it cannot be free. It is living within tension and attachment and therefore can never come into its fullest, most vibrant expression. So too, is the fate of a validation-based creative process. The imagination is stunted, and the humanity is dulled.

It wasn't until my final review as I prepared to graduate with my MFA in acting that the faculty unanimously offered glowing feedback of my work. I should have received that with tremendous gratitude, but all I felt was resentment that I hadn't received it sooner. This thought that if they told me more often that I was good enough, my work would be even better than it was.

I had placed far too much power in the hands of authority to validate my ability and ultimately grant me creative permission to do good work. It was my historical relationship to how I embodied and interacted with power and status that had kept me in my safe zone, which was one filled with defensiveness, arrogance, and isolationism. My habits of living a safe life limited me from untold creative awakening and significantly reduced my ability to embrace the not knowing, to celebrate the innate ability of my classmates, and to take full advantage of the wisdom of my instructors.

The relationship we build to status and power, our ability to trust our own status and power, and the equal ability to honor and receive the status and power of others, will deeply inform the way in which we are ultimately able to develop the behaviors of confidence.

A few years ago, I was in Berlin for a global change management conference where the topic was *Trust and Power or the Power of Trust*. I was surrounded by innovators in the change management space, fellow practitioners seeking to transform the human experience and bring a deeper level of compassion to organizational culture. I met people who specialized in trust, others who focused on belief, and still others who centered their work on communal thought or the science of decision-making. I, along with a colleague, brought a workshop exploring through game play the nature of status, perception, and unconscious power dynamics within relationship building. The goal of this particular conference was to—over the course of three days, numerous workshops, and beautifully facilitated group discussions—come up with what it meant to be a power that could be trusted. Namely, what behaviors someone in a position of power exhibited that lead to an experience of trust.

Three days of focused, rigorous discussion boiled down to three words: generosity, curiosity, and likability. That's it. So simple. It was not about physical strength, political advantage, or financial abundance. Trust of power comes down to qualities that stimulate safety, but also a willingness to adventure beyond. Generosity leading to loyalty. Curiosity leading to a motivating sense of wonder and possibility.

Likability leading to an overall experience of pleasantness within a power dynamic.

The three characteristics of a trusted power will also be found in someone perceived as confident or in ourselves when we are operating at our most authentic.

The behaviors behind confidence, mainly an easy body, open breath, and free voice, are witnessed in the authentic activation of power. We see this in great leaders. Some of the most influential leaders of our time are curious, generous, and likable. As people experiencing their leadership, we feel included, welcomed, encouraged, and at ease. We get the sense that they are listening deeply to us. They have a sincere desire to resolve problems or advance solutions. We feel safe and supported to explore, experiment, fail, and succeed.

What we are perceiving is confidence. What they are embodying is a distinct connection to breathing, effortless physical presence, and authentic vocalization. These qualities of power and leadership are not relegated to the elite few we, as a society, deem worthy of such accolade. Leadership can be present within the home, within your community, or within an organization.

What is within your control in this whole process is how you engage in the systems that surround you and the wise decisions you make regarding how to behave and negotiate status and power dynamics within those systems, including how you embody your own status and power.

I could not control the fact that the curriculum of my graduate training was redundant to me or that the other members of my class had received less prior training. I couldn't control the regularity or quality of the feedback I received from my instructors. What I could control was the quality with which I interacted in relationship to those circumstances. I was operating largely in arrogant behavior, full of tension, compromised breath, and inconsistent vocal presence.

What might have been if I were intentional in advocating for what was in my control? Breathing deeply, expressing effortlessly, and embracing the notion of "yes, and."

What Is Possible

It was the early '90s, and I really wanted to be cool. I was a product of the grunge movement and felt a deep connection to the alternative aesthetic. I was a regular at Sam Goody, always on the hunt for whatever paraphernalia they were hocking related to Stone Temple Pilots or The Smashing Pumpkins. I wore JNCO jeans and flannel shirts. The challenge was, I was a more dedicated fan of the aesthetic than the music (that wouldn't come until much later during my second music awakening #letheledout). So, although I knew who STP was, I couldn't recite the song titles from their debut album titled...I also didn't know the answer to that one. But I wanted to be cool. So, when I went to the local record store to comb through their tape selection, brought my treasures to check out, and the much cooler older townie scoffed, rolled his eyes, and said I should scratch that and check out Fugazi, I was like, "Oh totally. I've been meaning to do that." You are correct in assuming that I had not in fact ever heard of Fugazi up to that point, but I wanted this random dude to think I was cool.

This is just one of so many examples of when I lied to avoid feeling foolish. Did my feigned Fugazi knowledge have any implication on either of our well-beings? Save a deeper examination of the Butterfly Effect (the phenomenon whereby a minute localized change in a complex system can have large effects elsewhere), (Oxford Reference, 2022) I will venture to say, absolutely not. But these innocuous moments confront us all the time, right? Turmoil of adolescence aside, we are all subject to a desire to fit in or be liked or know the answer. At the moments when we are called to accept a reality that is outside of our lived experience, such as knowing who Fugazi is, we will typically make decisions to conform rather than deny. The impact of these micro-decisions is insignificant and largely inconsequential, but cumulatively have repercussions on the permission we grant ourselves to operate within our authenticity.

We begin to create muscle memory around behaviors of compliance rather than expand our potential to prepare to rise the call of "what if…"

Conformity is often the path of least resistance. I can completely understand the rationale of staying put. Of living the life you've been living because it's easier and familiar and the impact isn't honestly all that great. So, you have to lie once in a while, no big deal. You lie to yourself. You lie to your loved ones. You lie to strangers to ensure a decent enough first impression. And honestly, it's fine. You can make your way through life, never changing a thing, and you will probably die feeling perfectly okay. You didn't rock the boat, so you never experienced sea sickness. That is an accomplishment! It takes great commitment to safety to attach to a life of conformity and I applaud anyone who can actually rationalize that for their entire existence. As a person always on the edge of change, I often find myself fantasizing about falling back into a life of unconscious conformity.

You may live a rich fantasy life where you are a star quarterback in your fantasy football league, where you feel invincible. You may sing your little heart out while you're in the car, imagining a life where singing was what people knew you for, popstar notoriety to the max. You may sit at your desk, watching Janice walk right into the boss's office, ask for a promotion, and leave satisfied and aspire for that same life of opportunity, but never let it become more than a fantasy. Imagination is easy. Change is hard.

The only way transformation and growth can take place is by walking through the valley of change. There is no shortcut.

So, you decide, "Eh, never mind. It's fine. I like my imagination and that's good enough for me. I don't really care enough to do anything about that thing that inspires my imagination. I'll just let it exist as a fantasy." It's like when you're watching television and all of a sudden, you're dying for a snack. That little hunger pang rears its ugly head. But you're pretty cozy on the couch and Netflix just auto played another episode and so you just stay put, stomach growling. This goes on for hours. You accept the hunger because you just can't be bothered to get up off the couch. It's easy to justify, and I get it. Taking action can feel like a struggle not worth making. Conforming or taking the easier route is way more attractive than the route of challenge and change.

Not to mention, you are neurologically hardwired toward inertia. In her article published in *Psychology Today*, Amanda Habermann explains, "Our basal ganglia in the ancestral or primitive brain are responsible for 'wiring' habits. This cluster of nerve cell bodies is involved in functions such as automatic or routine behaviors (e.g., habits) that we are familiar with or that make us feel good. Such behaviors might include nail-biting, smoking cigarettes or following the same routine every day without making changes to it."

This part of the brain operates automatically, without much conscious decision-making involved. Habits serve a purpose. They make our day-to-day lives manageable and aid in survival. It is supported by, and often at odds with, the neocortex that controls conscious decision-making and takes far more effort to activate. Making decisions to not conform or shift behavior or incorporate new habits, all take tremendous conscious and concerted effort. The question you have to ask yourself is, in spite of all the obstacles, are you willing to give it a go?

Willpower leading to action is not necessarily a guaranteed formula.

Beyond the systems and the neurological pressures on you to conform to the status quo, there is also the matter of the ego. That self-conscious voice inside your head that, if left unchecked or under-nurtured, will prevent you from taking risks or embracing failure. The ego doesn't want to exist outside of conformity for fear of looking foolish.

I see this all the time in my workshops. I teach play to adults in suits. I ask senior leaders of powerful organizations to play games like Kitty Wants a Corner or Airplane, both of which require physical commitment outside the realm of normal activity, often paired with deep uncertainty and pressure to respond immediately or risk losing the game.

In these workshops, I witness the ego soften in real time. The game play usually begins with sincere hesitation or arrogance (fear disguised as overconfidence). Participants are standing in a circle, so there is nowhere to hide. They see everyone and everyone can see them. Even before the game play initiates, there is vast information around confidence levels reflected in their inability to simply stand still and await further instruction while sitting in a deep pool of uncertainty or anticipation. Grown men and women nervously crossing and uncrossing their arms, swaying from side to side or shifting their feet. Glances around the room, but complete resistance to make eye contact. Then the play begins.

The ego resistance shows up in not taking play seriously. They laugh at the silliness through a lens of judgment, confirmed by their side whispers and eye rolls. They half-heartedly engage their bodies in the actions required to succeed, leaving them safe because, if they don't try, they can't really fail. Then, suddenly, there is a shift. I see this pattern repeat itself from workshop to workshop, from group to group, all around the world. Participants see others enjoying themselves. They see laughter and mess ups and celebrations of close calls, resulting in failure. All of a sudden there is distinct permission to play because now their ego isn't on display. They become part of the collective experience and develop an overall behavior of surrender to the process, while maintaining autonomy and self-agency.

Surrender and self-awareness can coexist.

The ego can be understood, simplistically, as "me vs. other." It is a deep attachment to the safety of the self. Once an experience is universalized, normalized, or encouraged publicly, the ego implication is significantly lessened, and freedom of expression can now come fully into being. You are also empowered to grant yourself permission to soften the ego in the absence of collective permission. That is within your control, but, like much of what we're exploring, easier said than done.

Doing this on your own, outside of a group setting where you experience collective confidence, is challenging. Your brain is literally telling you to chill and not do anything outside of your comfort zone. It lets you know that what you're doing now is fine and that the risk you're thinking about taking is not really worth it. The brain starts its revolt in small ways by introducing limiting thoughts like "I can't" or "I shouldn't." If those signals are ignored, it kicks into high gear, activating the sympathetic nervous system, our fight-or-flight response. This is what is experienced in individuals with a crippling fear of public speaking. It's not a group activity. It's them against the world. The ego is at stake. The brain is short circuiting in this attempt at moving beyond the comfort zone. The body responds by shortening breath, limiting cognitive function, and diminishing access to physical and vocal expression. Everything in your immediate reality is screaming for you to retreat and get to safety. This is where you can step in to shepherd your body into surrender and activate confident behaviors that will put you and your lovely brain at ease.

Breath flow, body flow, brain flow, authenticity flow.

I was listening to the incomparable Krista Tippet interview Sharon Salzberg for her podcast, *On Being*. Salzberg, beyond being disarmingly relatable and cool and living deeply in what Krista refers to as her "hard won wisdom," is the co-founder of the Insight Meditation Society and credited as being one of the first to bring mediation to the west. I could write an entire book on what was discussed during this interview, but I want to focus on a key concept that Salzberg shares. She speaks at length, as is typical with a Buddhist meditation practice, about the notion of suffering. She reinforces a large component of this book's premise, which is that we cannot change our circumstances, but we can change our relationship of our experience to our circumstances. This is not novel. It is a foundation of Buddhist teaching. She promotes that if we are able to move outside of the suffering of our circumstances and witness them from outside of ourselves, we are now empowered to address them compassionately for ourselves and for others. She refers to our experience of the circumstances as "visiting forces."

Tremendous power lies in the notion of impermanence held within this description. There is also the idea that you are the owner of the property (mainly your mind) who is allowing or denying entry to these forces. This gives you full agency. At this point in the interview, I love when she shares that the "visiting forces" may come knocking, even relentlessly, but if you open the door to them and let them take over your house, you have lost sight of who actually lives there. (Tippet, 2021) What a powerful consideration. You are distinctly in the position of making a choice. There is also the inevitable suffering involved if, when you open the door to these "visiting forces" and then slam the door in their face, you will continue suffering through the lens of denial or resistance. This, of course, is experienced in the body as tension, held breath, affected vocalization, and risk aversion. Salzberg reduces, quite acutely, the experience and relationship to these "visiting forces" as making a choice and building practice around one moment:

"What do you do when you open the door?"

In my work as a confidence and communication coach and trainer, I refer to this moment when we open the door to visiting forces as the "precipice of truth." The moment when you are called to rise to the occasion and just as quickly confronted with the deep chasm of fear, that moment when the "visiting forces" of self-doubt come knocking at your door. When that moment inevitably arrives, do you slam the door shut and deny their existence? Do you let them in to take over your home? Or do you welcome them, give them a cup of coffee, and send them on their way? Breath flow, body flow, brain flow, authenticity flow. Ideas and feelings and experiences will come knocking. The visitors will not cease attempting to gain access to your mind, but you can allow them to be a part of the flow. You can breathe them in and release them on the exhale. That is within your control.

The confident body is one that allows the experience and circumstance of suffering, the self-defeating thoughts or self-aggrandizing behavior, to become a part of the natural order. And when you are called to action, when the moment comes to rise to the occasion, the confident body will remain open to breath, easy in body, and expressive in voice. Not through denial of circumstance, but rather through an acceptance of circumstance, free from attachment. From this place, the confident body, having opened the door to these "'visiting forces," can then move into presence and catapult itself across the threshold of fear. This is the moment of decision when you confront the precipice of truth. It is a similar reflection of "what do you do when you open the door?" When called to rise to the occasion, be it for a high stakes presentation or simply to tell someone you love them for the first time, do you advance in authenticity or retreat in fear?

The threshold of truth is the barrier of freedom. That is the power of living in a confident body.

It is not a perfect system. You cannot control the process to a predictable degree of perfection. You will be caught off guard. You will, at times, be overcome by the "visiting forces." You will have moments where you move out of presence or put on a protective layer of inauthenticity. We are complex beings; therefore, it must stand to reason that the journey will be riddled with complexity. The complexity will show up in your emotions and how you negotiate your relationship to historic systems and circumstances that no longer serve you. Complexity will come in the form of relearning how you understand your breathing or relationship to your body. What is not complex and a foundation that you can always come back to is the breath itself.

The breath will be a constant access point for presence and compassion, both for self and others. It is the tether amid the chaos.

I want to quickly address what we have covered before initiating the more explicit exploration of habits and behaviors. We have become aware that systems exist outside of our control and often even without our conscious awareness. We have awoken to these systems and defined what is within our control to support us in operating in deep authenticity within those systems. We understand that throughout this process of unlocking our full potential, we will be confronted with strong desires both externally and internally to reclaim the status quo, stay in the safe zone, and opt for easy over authentic. This is not a speculation. It is a certainty. Allow all your thoughts and feelings to emerge as you move through the following chapters of addressing, releasing, and rebuilding habits of confidence. Then immediately place your attention on your breath, your body, and the incredible power of authentic expression that is already inside of you, waiting to be unleashed. Let's go.

IMAGINE

Benefits of Discomfort

Show of hands, who has a gym membership that they signed up for one early spring morning after realizing beach season was right around the corner, so you better get off your butt and get your body back in shape, only to never darken the doorway, save the one time you went to get your key tag? I have spent so many moments thinking, "I should go to the gym today," only to forget literally fifteen seconds later when I distract myself with something that feels far more essential, like organizing my closet. I have a spark of sensation in my body that says, "You are capable of incredible things, and you should build strength to ensure vitality and longevity!" And just like that, a new thought enters, and the gym becomes but a distant memory of an impulse gone unanswered.

Don't get me wrong; I love physical activity. I taught kickboxing for years, practice ashtanga yoga regularly, and go running several times a week. Where I experience resistance to the gym is in the lack of familiarity. My brain resists the impulse because not only is it not a habit, but it's also unknown. I don't know the people there. I don't know the machines. It's a new environment, and I don't know what to expect when I walk in. What will the vibe be? Will people stare at me? How much sweat is too much sweat? Will the machines be opened to use or will it be so busy that I will have to wait, standing around like some dork, attempting to look like I belong there? I've even gone so far as to map my run to pass by the gym and just keep running once I reach the intersection.

I experience this same level of resistance in so many areas of my life. I am a single woman living in Brooklyn. I travel the world by myself. I navigate cities all over the world solo, but still the idea of adventuring out on my own is arresting. It requires me to take risks alone, inspire myself, and encourage myself all without any safety net of support, reassurance, or familiarity. I will go out for a walk (one of my favorite activities) with the intention to eventually find a spot to get a beer or a bourbon, depending on the season. I cannot tell you how many times I have walked around for over an hour, peeking into local watering holes, only to decide, without even walking inside, that it's too busy and I would just be the weirdo sitting at the bar by myself.

On the other hand, there's the comfort of my local bar, where I am a regular. I don't have the same challenge of familiarity. Even on trivia Tuesdays, when I am surrounded by groups of friends, I will sit solo at the bar and not have any sense of resistance or discomfort. I won't even look at my phone! I'll just sit there. Thinking, observing, eavesdropping, having a chat with the bartender, but mainly minding my own business. I feel at home there. It is within my comfort zone.

It's part of my daily practice to challenge this comfort zone. To test my boundaries in order to grow; to embrace the experience of adversity. Adversity is what we are experiencing in the moment when we approach the outer edge of our comfort zone. I have become intimately familiar with the experience of adversity and consider it a fundamental part of the process toward developing confident behavior, but that wasn't always the case.

There have been countless times I have made excuses not to attend a party at the last minute because the idea of showing up to a place full of strangers was just too overwhelming. I am largely an introvert, and my nature defies my intention, so I must push through that "natural" state and embrace being uncomfortable. That tickle of anxiety, that fear, as I leave what feels safe. The challenge begets the reward.

What would happen if we never experienced adversity? If we never exited the confines of our safety zone?

Eckhart Tolle has a beautiful way of speaking to the importance of adversity's role in the process of conscious awakening. In an interview with Oprah, he frames adversity as a necessity, not only as a primary driver of evolution, but the key component in developing conscious and valuable humans. Reflecting on the evolution of flight, he says, "For every life form, life is a challenge. If it were not, they would not evolve. I am sure the reason why certain animals can fly, is there was a need for them. If they had not been able to overcome gravity, they would not have survived." (Tolle, 2021)

There must have been tremendous experience of adversity in the environment and circumstance of certain birds to compel them to seek flight. It was adversity that drove evolution. Similarly, when it comes to the evolution of human consciousness, adversity is necessary to transcend the experience of suffering of the ego. Every time we experience adversity, our ego diminishes, and our consciousness creates a deeper foundation of wisdom, ultimately leading to transcendence into a deep spiritual awakening.

Getting uncomfortable is the most fundamental aspect of any personal development journey and a primary driver for living in a confident body.

In my kickboxing days, during the conditioning portion of class where we would do burpees and core work and more push-ups than should ever be required by a regular human and the muscles are burning and everything in your scope of consciousness is screaming to stop and grab a nap, the trainers would declare to the room, "Pain is weakness leaving the body!" If Eckhart Tolle didn't inspire with his theory of conscious awakening through adversity, perhaps this fitness themed mantra will suffice.

Our bodies do not want to pick up heavy things, sweat, strain, and put them back down again. The experience of this adversity to the muscles and our mind is one of sincere resistance. However, it is through this process of adversity that we develop strong and vital bodies that aid in our ability to move through life with better health. Not to mention, the process of overcoming adversity and getting uncomfortable actually produces more energy for the body, thereby making the adversity seem less severe. We eventually acclimate to the other side of our comfort zone.

The chaos we feel in the moments of growth or change ultimately rediscovers order, and we come back into balance with stronger layers of resilience and adaptability.

It's important to test the boundaries of your comfort zone and build up a tolerance to discomfort. Stepping outside of your comfort zone and embracing uncharted territory can only happen if you know where comfort ends and discomfort begins. I picture my farm growing up. We had large pastures behind the house that moved upward on a gentle slope, backing up to a small forest. Your comfort lives in the pastures. What would it feel like to cross the boundary into the forest? Begin by asking yourself, where do you feel safe? Where do you feel the presence of risk? Where lies the threshold of fear?

A roadmap for getting uncomfortable:

1. Build a practice of observation.

Observe when your body responds with resistance to a situation or interactions. For me, that may look like the act of going to a party by myself or expressing romantic feelings for a crush who hasn't necessarily indicated the feeling will be mutual. For you, that may look like singing karaoke or walking through a crowded street or the act of saying no to someone who constantly violates your boundaries.

Testing your comfort zone is like testing the temperature of water. You don't put your whole hand under the faucet to see if it's hot. You start with one finger. It is easy to become overwhelmed by the enormity of taking risks. We can become paralyzed at the largest of the unknown. So, start small, without any expectation.

2. Get curious about where you feel most like yourself and inspired by your surroundings.

Stepping outside of your comfort zone in the process of unlocking your full potential is not about forcing you into things outside the realm of your authenticity. We are not inviting discomfort for discomfort's sake. It is about expanding the boundary of potential around those things that light you up. This is important. Everything is not for everyone. Jumping out of a plane, for example, is outside of my comfort zone. My body rejects all consideration of that as an activity. I will go on record as saying that I will never jump out of a plane, much to the chagrin of a good friend of mine who is an expert skydiver. There are plenty of methods for expanding my comfort zone, but seeking adrenaline with a parachute is not one that appeals to me or is ultimately in service of the transformation I am seeking.

A great example of this would be the time I performed stand-up comedy when I was in college. It was a summer course focused on the history of New York City comedy, and our final project was to perform stand-up at the Broadway Comedy Club. Even as an actress in training, this felt way outside my comfort zone. It was a huge risk, but it aligned to where I felt most authentic and directly supported my desire to expand and move beyond comfort toward a deeper level of potential. I was feeling resistance to delivering my stand-up routine right up until the moment they called my name, but I leaped across the threshold of fear and came out on the other side more capable and with greater capacity for weathering adversity and discomfort than before.

3. Commit to the act of expanding your comfort zone.

Observing without action is just daydreaming. We are in search of meaningful and lasting behavior change.

Like stand-up for me, what is something that you can begin to test your comfort level around? Lean into what lights you up. This has the potential to invite in new relationships, establish deeper learning about something you are passionate about, or bestow on you the experience of coming face to face with an invigorating feeling of aliveness. Leaning into what feels authentic and lights you up will allow you to get comfortable with getting uncomfortable. It will diminish the level of intimidation or perceived consequence you may feel around initiating the process of stepping outside of your comfort zone.

Getting uncomfortable does not mean cloaking yourself in discomfort. It is simply a call to action to stretch yourself in ways that will only serve to increase your presence toward your experience of this one life you are conscious to. Do you want to watch from the sidelines, or do you want to be an active player in the game of your life?

A proposed series of challenges to expand your comfort zone:

- Take yourself out to dinner alone

- Do ten jumping jacks and make a loud squawk when your hands go up

- Join an improv class (they have many virtual options now, so you can find a class no matter where you are in the world)

- Call someone (not text) that you haven't spoken to in a while, just to say hi

- Film yourself with your phone camera singing "Twinkle, Twinkle, Little Star" and send it to five people

- Create your own authentic discomfort challenge

The practice of expanding your comfort zone by way of the topic or activity that lights you up will lead to the desired personal transformation and, let's face it, be a lot more fun along the way.

A simple decision to advance and expand in an area that aligns with your authenticity has a tremendous reverberating effect. It starts with the idea, the idea moves into strategy and conscious decision, those conscious decisions will inevitably take you on a journey of self-discovery and expression of your full potential.

Truth Telling

I am going to tell you a story about acting, but I first want to remind you what acting is. Acting is not pretending. Acting, at its core, is truth telling. It is authenticity in the most intentional form. The sole job of the actor is to stand bravely and tell the truth in the face of extraordinary circumstances. This is also what we are called to do as regular people in moments of challenge or change. At the Atlantic Theater Company where I trained as an actress, we conducted ourselves under a simple premise: "Invent nothing. Deny nothing." This is the job of the actor and the goal of our work together as regular people walking through the journey of life.

I was taking part in a summer retreat with the Atlantic Theater Company hosted at the University of Vermont in Burlington. It was an intensive three-week program where we would incubate and advance the skills of script analysis, breath, and bodywork, and acting technique. We were fortunate to have incredible minds of the theater present and willing to guide us into a deeper capacity for truth telling.

Besides David Mamet making a guest appearance, which was accompanied by a lot of fanfare and admiration as the father of the technique we were studying, we also had the distinct fortune to be instructed in our scene study work by Scott Zigler, one of the coauthors of the Practical Aesthetic, supervisor for IATT at Harvard University and current Dean of Drama for UNCSA. Scott has a seemingly effortless way of encouraging creative expression and fostering such simplicity and honesty in the work of acting. There is no ego, even for such an accomplished director. He is fully present to the task of helping you reveal your truth using only yourself and the words on the page. One class in particular, we were working with the text of Chekhov. I was assigned a scene from *Ivanov* playing the role of Anna, the wife who is emotionally neglected by Ivanov (her husband) and is currently dying of tuberculosis.

This is why I love my acting technique. How on earth could I possibly pretend to have tuberculosis or trick myself into becoming a dying character from prewar Moscow? Acting is not faking it until you make it. What my technique encourages is to understand the objective behind the scene, layer on any required externals almost like a prop (in this case severe bouts of coughing), and pursue the objective until it has been achieved, even in the face of inevitable failure. That's it. You are not cloaked in the character. You are you.

"Invent nothing. Deny nothing."

My scene partner and I were awaiting our turn to share our work and receive feedback from Scott. We waited and waited. Ours was the final scene to go up that day, and we were left with only twenty minutes to perform, receive notes, and try to incorporate the notes (a standard structure for scene study). I was feeling discouraged because this was a three-hour class. Other scenes had received over forty-five minutes of focused instruction. I felt like we couldn't possibly get the same benefit in less than half the time. We began our scene, which is the culminating scene in Act Three where Anna, in her compromised state of health, confronts Ivanov about a supposed affair.

I was just nineteen at the time. I had never been in a real relationship, much less experienced the betrayal of an affair. Nor had I ever been stricken with a major illness or had any sincere awareness of how tuberculosis impacted the body, beyond the coughing fits. What I did have was my objective—to get my husband to right a terrible wrong. The scene plays out, and it's...fine. We did exactly what we set out to do. The blocking all came together. We hit the important points in the arch of the scene, displaying the appropriate emotion. Scott took a moment before offering his feedback, all of us waiting in mild suspense, when he finally spoke and directed us to simply "do it again, but faster." He was usually so full of wisdom and insight, and now all he had for us was to speed it up. So, that's what we did. And it was one of the most truthful and visceral acting moments of my career.

What Scott had identified was that all the elements were there. Clear intention, clear understanding of the scene and circumstances. But what was missing was truth, the revelation of the humanity of the characters. Our first presentation was acceptable but controlled. We were working very hard to hit all the expected points and do a "good job," but not surrender to the immediacy of the moment. We weren't telling the truth. We were manufacturing the truth.

In the second run of the scene, by simply moving more quickly, increasing the need in moments, we were no longer able to control each moment, but rather had to commit fully to what was happening directly in front of us and stay present to the immediacy of the unfolding in real time. There was no time for manufacturing. We invented nothing and denied nothing. The scene was alive and sincere and invigorating. This was my most lucid moment of understanding the power and potential of speaking my truth. Confidence, like good acting, can only be present when truth is the main ingredient. What we perceive or experience when truth is present can be most directly identified as authenticity.

Authenticity is the experience of truth, both in receiving and in expressing.

Truth and authenticity are interdependent. One cannot exist without the other. When taken out of a scene study class and applied to real life, we experience truth as an acute alignment to an essential need. The reason I was able to experience such presence in that scene is because I was moving and expressing not as Anna, but as myself, liberated from constraint of what I perceived as appropriate or the right way to conduct the scene. I simply allowed myself to pursue my objective and be driven by an essential need. What brings truth to life and into the realm of authenticity is a purpose behind the truth telling—the action of speaking up.

Authenticity, similar to confidence, is a perception. We are witnessing authenticity. What you are doing is truth telling. This, of course, begs the question, what do we mean by truth? How can we determine if we are speaking our truth, especially if we are operating under a veil of unconscious conditioning, predisposed to conform rather than speak up?

Truth, in the context of confident behavior, is not the expression of words or the righteousness of a distinct philosophy. Truth is driven by the need to speak, not by an idea of what needs to be said. Truth is what happens when you honor an impulse brought about by sincere listening and connection to breath. It is the impulse connected to the inhale, the moment of inspiration. Inhale to inspire, exhale to express. The impulse of truth, that moment of inspiration, can be described as a bubble of energy, the spark of yes.

Truth is the experience of absolute honesty, the intuitive certainty of energetic alignment.

If we translate this into the scene in Vermont, once we sped up and relinquished control, we were able to exist simply in the space of inhale and exhale, the flow of deep listening. We could only be responsive to the cycle of inspire → express, inspire → express. We trusted the impulse to drive our moment-to-moment interaction. We knew where we were going. The scene was all laid out. What kept it alive, immediate, and unpredictable (even amid the predictability) was our willingness to stay open and responsive to how the impulse guided us to our final destination.

It is important to identify that truth telling is not free of compassionate awareness. Authenticity holds self-advocacy and awareness of others in simultaneous focus at all times. Truth telling without strategy or objective is about you and your ego. Truth telling with strategy and objective is about a sincere negotiation of relationship in service of others as well as yourself.

I share this direction with my clients: "Live your truth, speak your truth, be your truth, unapologetically all time, as long as it's coming from love." It all comes down to living deeply in your truth, while holding a heavy emphasis on the fact that you are in this world and of this world. Authenticity presumes emotional intelligence. This means being responsive to the impact of your actions and behaviors on the world around you. Without it, you're just a jerk walking through life thinking the rules don't apply to you. Truly authentic people know how to play well with others and how to invite others to play with them.

In the realm of the real world, it takes courage to tell the truth.

This does not have to be verbal. Again, we are not asserting our ideas onto the world. Truth telling is an energetic expression or exchange. It can be present in silence and stillness. Truth telling is allowing the impulse to be felt as well as heard. It is honoring intuition. Listening and being responsive to the spark of yes is a necessary aspect of truth telling, but one of the most challenging aspects to commit to and embody in the practice of confident behavior.

One of my clients recently described her experience of denying her truth as feeling as if she has a pit in her stomach. She talks about it as a pit because she resisted the spark of yes. The impulse had become hardened and solid rather than vibrant and flowing. She was aware of the impulse and of the desire, but she contained it. In containing that energy that wanted to be expressed, her body responded in tension filled ways. She held her breath. She made way for the judging mind and fell into the chasm of self-defeat. Her body was literally translating this resistance as anxiety or fear. What happened in the scene in Vermont is we were releasing the impulse. It felt free. It felt alive and connected. It didn't feel resistant or controlled.

When you resist your truth, it shows up in your body in ways that feel like you're trying to hold it hostage.

The most challenging moment of truth telling is the moment of release. To make the choice to leap across the chasm of uncertainty. To cross the threshold of fear.

Telling the truth happens in three parts:

1. acknowledging the spark of yes

2. taking action to release that impulse, to honor the moment of ignition

3. committing to the expression of the impulse toward completion

If these stages are honored, it will feel like a mild catharsis instead of a pit in your stomach. You have now released this little bit of pent-up tension or resistance. When you tell the truth, your body feels at ease and comes back into stasis. What allows the truth to be honored is a connection to breath, openness of body, and freedom of expression in body and voice. But, like the rest of our confidence journey, it will be an imperfect process riddle with inevitable failure.

I have another client who came to me with a distinct desire to become a better storyteller. Not only did he want to tell impactful stories, but he also wanted to be able to invite storytelling into unplanned moments. To build the habit of mental agility and creative adaptability. This required a connection to breath (inspiration) and a willingness to honor the spark of yes. The first stage of this process was exercising the imagination and building the skill of association using the tool of "as if." This is a common tool I recommend when dealing with complicated and challenging content or ideas. The "as if" brings the complex into a space of relatability through the use of a parallel, and often more pedestrian, related scenario. My client really responded to the tool of "as if." He first had to exercise his brain to re-invite imagination and narrative association. This innate experience of play had become dormant on his journey to adulthood. We had to reawaken this intuitive response.

The next step was practicing implementing the tool of "as if" into conversations with familiar and low-stakes relationships. At a family dinner, for example. This entire process was one of conscious redirection. He was observing and making deliberate choices to embrace the philosophy of "I wonder what would happen if..." Once he readapted to responding to the impulse of imagination and storytelling, to allow his body to inspire his mind, he then opened up to exploring the tool in a professional environment.

He made the decision, which was outside of his comfort zone, to cross that threshold of fear and start telling a story in a place where he had never told a story before—in a presentation to a number of key stakeholders. I was so proud of him for having the courage to honor the spark of yes. He explained the experience as if he just all of a sudden had this idea of an "as if" and went with it. (The experience of truth telling can be that simple.) He saw something in the presentation deck that made him think of this old cartoon "Goofus and Gallant." But as he started to tell the story, as he was channeling this impulse to his audience, he started to negate that impulse. He started to second guess himself. He still went through the story, but he was kind of fumbling because now he was overthinking it. He was trying to control the flow as opposed to allow the flow. He wasn't trusting the impulse to drive his need to speak or trusting that the connection to his truth would allow his thoughts to be communicated effectively.

Speaking should be as easy as breathing.

After the presentation, he felt like he hadn't done a good job. Ultimately, he realized that the experience of "not doing a good job" was a result of him not fully honoring the impulse and allowing that impulse to be expressed fully. He had tried to manufacture or manipulate the way the impulse presented itself. He backed off of the truth. He stopped trusting the "as if" halfway through. If he had continued to trust his impulse and release it mindfully, consciously, not recklessly, but strategically, he could have ended with a feeling of completion.

After unpacking the moment-to-moment unfolding of this experience, we identified that a couple moments into the story he had started to welcome in the judging and controlling mind. The self-conscious mind is guided by the ego, which carries with it fear of rejection, judgment, and risk aversion. He began to hold his breath and disconnect from his need to speak, as well as from his audience. In the middle of his "as if" narrative, he started to think it was too abstract and not interesting enough. As a result, he started to manipulate the story to become less saturated and more diluted. The impulse, the moment of ignition, held the point. In the controlling of or retreating from the impulse, his point was no longer driving him and as a result he started to fumble his words. The need was lost. He had become self-conscious. The energy and vibration of the truth had not been fully released, and he was now left with a sensation of incompletion. This feeling of not doing a good job was his way of expressing a residue of inauthenticity. He did not experience his truth fully, nor did he allow his audience to have the experience of truth. As a result, everyone was left feeling incomplete.

Telling the truth is a willingness to say yes.

You must embrace a willingness to get inspired and to express yourself. To listen deeply, respond with purpose, and pursue the need to speak with full commitment. It is allowing yourself to play fully and freely, while ensuring that you are able to play fully and freely with others. Telling your truth will allow you to thrive in the face of uncertainty. Telling your truth will bring you back to life.

Inevitable Vulnerability

I'm sitting here for the third day in a row, staring at my computer, trying to write this freaking chapter. I sit down, write a few partially coherent thoughts, get distracted, prioritize other things, and all of a sudden, I have a social life I need to attend to and the chapter remains unwritten—at home, alone, while I am out procrastinating. It's Saturday night, I'm sitting at my desk, and it finally occurred to me to ask the most obvious question: "Why am I struggling to write the chapter on vulnerability?" Lightbulb.

Let's break down the facts. I am currently in the midst of a deeply vulnerable process, writing a book about my life's work. I am struggling to substantiate my business in a new way after a global pandemic. I am, in any direction I look, face to face with vulnerability, and if I spend too long in the conscious presence of that vulnerability, the plates stop spinning and I lose it all.

I am a perfectionist in "cool girl" clothes, and I have a propensity toward self-sabotage. I do this so that when the thing, whatever the thing is at the moment that feels of the utmost importance inevitably fails, there won't be that much hurt because I didn't try that hard anyway. Feeling the pressure of writing this book, the immensity of putting myself out there, I realize that I'm trying to stop it before it's even had a chance to succeed. This pattern repeats itself. It is my way of staying safe.

But I will never escape the call or threat of vulnerability, and neither can you. We're constantly confronted with vulnerability. We are always living on the precipice of change, living on the precipice of the opportunity to finally speak our truth, and deciding whether to retreat or advance. The only constant is change, and it's vulnerable as hell. That's the feeling I have right now. Everything is vulnerable, and I am experiencing vulnerability heavily in my body. What a tremendous opportunity for self-reflection and deep consideration for what vulnerability actually means, both in thought and feeling. How does it show up in action? How does it show up in relationships? How does it show up in the body?

Vulnerability is inescapable, so perhaps we should embrace it as a part of our given circumstance.

Vulnerability can show up in ways like asking for a raise, coming out to your parents, or standing up for yourself when someone cuts you in line. This level of vulnerability is riddled with potential emotional consequence. It is elective vulnerability. But vulnerability is also inherent in nature. All things on this earth are vulnerable to the elements, cosmic forces, and the unstoppable process of evolution. Vulnerability can be embraced as the natural order, an unavoidable certainty, and essential to our experience as humans on this earth. We can empower ourselves to lower the stakes on vulnerability and embrace the wisdom it is trying to teach us.

I was fifteen years old, walking through the halls of my high school, likely heading to inspect the status of the recycling bins. I was president of the ecology club and a relentless advocate for proper school wide adherence to recycling guidelines. The layout of my high school was quirky. It was built in 1884 and has been expanded over the years with various new wings and additions. This makes for a bygone era aesthetic with a whimsical call for adventure and imagination. It also means there are a multitude of small connecting sets of steps. One step down here. Three steps down there. I was coming through a short hallway connecting the oldest building with a newer building. As I was passing the auditorium and rounding the corner to make my way down a short set of steps, I miscalculated my footing and began to fall.

I fell so slowly. I remember being conscious of the imminence of a misstep, so I tried to regain balance preemptively. This took my torso back, but my feet kept going. When my foot landed on a step, two steps down, my torso was propelled forward. I attempted to align myself and stand up straight, or at least regain balance, but to no avail. I fell. I fell hard. And I fell slowly. Not a slow-motion, cinematic flashback fall, but a real-life slow fall. Right in front of the welcome area where several people waited, watching this happen. Did I mention I was wearing a skirt?

It is in remembering such pedestrian foibles (pun intended) that I am graciously reminded of the fact that, in spite of our most extraordinary effort to meet perfection and become immune to failing, we will never succeed. Simply because our effort is matched and exceeded by a simple truth, we are subject to laws of the universe and constantly vulnerable to the perils of gravity and balance.

Vulnerability is built into nature. It is built into our nature. Unfortunately, so too is our ego and self-conscious capacity for fear.

Maslow's hierarchy of needs places the need to fortify against the elements as our most basic level of need—shelter, water, sleep, food. At the top of the hierarchy is the need for belonging and a sense of purpose. As humans, in pursuit of our most self-actualized expression of being, lives the desire to feel seen and heard. We dedicate tremendous amounts of psychic and emotional energy to trying to be seen and heard. On the other side of that effort is the energy spent on fearing not being seen and heard. (Maslow, 1943) That is the space of vulnerability.

What if we accept our personal vulnerability in the same way that we accept environmental vulnerability? There is a strong likelihood you will succumb to the powers of gravity and balance. There is an equally strong likelihood that someone will misunderstand you or not acknowledge you in the way you desire to be seen. You will go for a hug when the other person goes for a handshake. You will spill wine at your partner's parent's fancy dinner party. You will wave back at that attractive person waving at you, only to realize they are waving to the person behind you. These are the unavoidable laws of nature.

We can, however, develop resilience to vulnerability. We can allow vulnerability to become a conscious part of our experience without allowing the associated emotional impact to overtake us. This takes courage. Intentionally activating vulnerability through exposure to risk is a gutsy move. When's the last time you were intentionally silly or invited looking foolish? It's not something we do with gusto, but it does take guts.

We become afraid of vulnerability when we resist it, rather than become resilient in the face of it.

Resistance is a denial of the presence of vulnerability. A hardening of oneself against vulnerability, making us impervious to feelings of uncertainty, failure, or hurt, while simultaneously hardening ourselves to love and joy and belonging. It is in direct contention with our desire to be seen and heard. Resistance prevents others from really seeing us and prevents us from speaking out truth. Resilience is welcoming and a releasing. Resistance is denying and withdrawing.

In her Netflix special *The Call to Courage*, Brené Brown tells simple and meaningful stories of how she experiences vulnerability in her own life in the same way she has seen it reflected time and time again in her research. These moments where we are confronted with wanting to be accepted, seen, and heard. When our heart is on the line. When our self-identity is at stake. When our perceived value is in question.

The way we respond to these vulnerabilities is remarkable. Our little bodies and brains will do whatever it takes to make sense of a situation, and this often means falling back into historic trauma patterns and self-sabotaging narrative. Brown identifies these patterns in such a beautifully relatable way in what she refers to as her "magic sentence." When she realizes she is falling down a spiral into the dark chasm of self-defeat (this is how I refer to the moment we are swept up in anxious thoughts), Brown clicks back into presence and identifies the narrative habit as simply "the story I am telling myself." How powerful is that? These stories are not based on reality. They are based on fear, fantasy, and deep vulnerability.

I can totally relate to this idea of "story." It's like when you are waiting on a call from a new crush because they totally said they would call and they're not calling, and you go to sleep, and they still haven't called. You lay your head on the pillow, but your mind is racing, playing out all of the scenarios of what could have possibly happened (mugged, sick, forgot about me, lost phone...) only to land on the most elaborate and self-defeating solution, which is probably akin to "they are with someone else they like more and are ghosting me, and I will never hear from them again." Then you wake up to a text late at night apologizing with a clear and reasonable explanation for the delay. Your anxiety subsides, and you go to sleep.

These stories can be elaborate or simple but are most often based on trauma rather than reality. Mine right now is, "Everyone will think I am a fraud and scoff at my arrogant attempt to write a book on confidence." I am aware of the irony in such an unconfident narrative. When I sit with this vulnerability and allow it to engulf me, I feel it living in my shoulders, which are rolled forward and bringing me into a diminished, low-status posture. My breath is held, and my gaze is withdrawn. My overall physical experience is one of retraction. This reaction is reminiscent of so many moments in my life, a pattern that repeats itself. So, let me ask you:

- What is a story you tell yourself?

- Is there a consistent theme to the story you tell yourself?

- Is it representative of your need to stay safe and remain entrenched in historic patterns that no longer serve you?

- How does this experience of vulnerability live in your body?

Brown defines vulnerability for us as the experience of uncertainty, risk, or emotional exposure. Going off of this definition, it then stands to reason, and Brown supports this in her research, that the key ingredient for embracing vulnerability, for crossing that threshold of fear, is courage. The ability to step into risk and uncertainty despite signals and stories telling you to retreat and stay safe. The courage to interrupt the story you are telling yourself, to catapult yourself across the threshold of fear, into the valley of transformation, and in service of tapping hidden potential.

This practice of activating courage will embed resilience into the experience of vulnerability.

Speaking up in gratitude is a great way to practice courage and vulnerability. It puts you in an offer versus ask dynamic, which can feel more emotionally manageable. In short, simple, direct language, communicate your experience of gratitude to another person. Do it intentionally in feedback sessions or planned conversation or extemporaneously when you have an impulse of gratitude. I send voice messages to my team whenever they simply occur to me outside of any direct communication on a project status update. I feel really energized after, and my team appreciates the unsolicited acknowledgment.

Often, we negate the impulse to speak up in gratitude as not important, or not a priority, or you don't want to bother them, whomever they are. But I'll urge you to consider that what is really driving the negation of the impulse and expression of gratitude is our fear of being vulnerable. It's like telling someone you like them and face the potential of having them respond with a blank stare. It's an icky feeling. It touches the deepest parts of us. The depths of our experience that have been with us and created the lens through which we exist in this world—our patterns, behaviors, beliefs about ourselves and others.

Being vulnerable is against our primal nature, when in fact it is the key to survival today. Vulnerability and driving with the behaviors of confidence, authenticity, and emotional intelligence will transform our lives and redefine culture to meet the shifting ethos of human interaction. An article from Harvard Health Publishing titled "Giving thanks can make you happier" found that "in positive psychology research, gratitude is strongly and consistently associated with greater happiness. Gratitude helps people feel more positive emotions, relish good experiences, improve their health, deal with adversity, and build strong relationships." It allows you, in the process of acknowledging the feeling of gratitude, to identify what you positively respond to and the types of circumstances that elicit ease and alignment, allowing for a greater likelihood of authentic interaction.

Speaking up in gratitude carries inherent uncertainty and requires courage and commitment to follow through. But what a meaningful practice to undertake. You are giving someone a gift of being seen as well as practicing standing behind what you like, dislike, and value. For example,

"I appreciate your patience" tells the person that you respect their time and also informs you that time and respect are important to you.

"Thank you for the clear feedback" tells the person that you are honoring them through hearing and receiving their thoughts and feelings, while giving you insight that external reflection is valuable for your growth.

"It's important to me to acknowledge how much I appreciate your initiative" lets the person know you see and value their loyalty and commitment, while affirming for you that feeling support through acts of service is a motivating and necessary for a feeling of collaboration.

Like everything else we have explored, vulnerability takes practice. Patsy Rodenburg writes in her book, *The Second Circle*, "We can block our hearts as effectively as we can block our minds. Guilt, shame, and fear can rapidly shift you out of your presence. This shift is an initial and natural reaction in order to bury, deny, or ridicule the emotion." I want you to think back to a vulnerable moment in your life, like a first date, a public speaking moment, or even just receiving a heartfelt compliment in front of other people. Notice the swell of reaction as you had that experience of vulnerability. It rises from the bottom up. You are welcome to all that comes along with that feeling. That experience of trigger in the body, the unprompted slideshow of hurt that it potentially creates in the mind, the way it impacts how you interact with anyone present.

You have a choice in this moment to maintain presence or shift away from presence, to make a choice in the moment before you react. There are two options before you: 1) You can experience any feeling that emerges and meet that feeling with fear, possibly disguised as anger, defensiveness, or collapse, or 2) You can have that feeling and meet it with recognition of the feeling and surrender to make way for presence and compassion. You can make your way through the fear by grounding yourself in your breath, taking a moment to release the body from protective tension, and proceed in a confident body. This is how you teach your body to cross the threshold of fear. To become resilient rather than resistant.

You must embrace and honor the experience of vulnerability as a clue for transformation.

Have you ever seen someone really distraught and trying to speak? Maybe you've experienced that for yourself. I know I have. Distress can be severe, a reaction to the news of a deceased loved one, for example. It can also be mild, addressing a misunderstanding between two friends. The body prepares and responds to distress by inviting tension. This impacts the breath and ultimately the voice. Voice is a symptom of the body. In these moments of distress, there is a predictable pattern of physical behavior where first the body resists the enormity of feeling through held breath, tense muscles in the shoulders and throat, and avoidant eye contact. Then the body will soften and relinquish to the experience of distress, and through the relinquishing comes release. The muscles soften around the throat, the breath is reclaimed (often heard through a strong exhale or audible sigh), and eye contact is reintroduced in an attempt to reconnect to the environment.

You can hear the impact of distress and resistance in the voice, or maybe you can remember this for yourself. That feeling of being "all choked up" or having a "frog in your throat." Fighting through tears can manifest through vocal constraint. The body is holding. After the body relinquishes, the distraught person may still be experiencing and even expressing strong emotion, but their voice is now freer to communicate with intention. This is a predictable physiological pattern. The vulnerability in staying available to the process itself is substantial.

To honor your experience of distress while still moving forward with purpose—that takes courage.

As you move through these practices, you will also be confronted with intellectual vulnerability. We are creatures that desire order. When we are in the chaos of uncertainty, we lose our foundation of safety. There will be questions that emerge or a deep desire to understand quickly or to get it right. In the moment where you consciously register feelings of intellectual vulnerability in the body, often indicated by held or shallow breathing and a restriction in the throat, direct your attention from the mind back to the body. Ground your feet. Bring your attention to the length and release of the spine. Embrace the space of not knowing. It is the void between what has been and what will be. It is the present moment. You cannot zoom out and attempt to intellectually know how your body will ultimately experience cultivating the tool of resilience versus resistance. You must stay open to the emergence of this behavior without a predetermination of how this behavior will manifest. That will lead to a more authentic expression of the behavior and ultimately one that will allow you to feel at ease even in the face of adversity and inevitable moments of vulnerability.

Body and Breath

How often do you stop to celebrate your body? Sometimes I will be walking around my neighborhood and have a simple thought like, "My knees are so amazing to just bend and straighten, aiding in propelling me forward." I will run up a steep hill and feel my breath heaving in my chest and quickly return to stasis once I reach the top, where I will consciously register the gift of my ability to develop physical fitness. This body is my vessel for carrying me through this one life I am conscious to. Bodies create new blood cells, fend off disease, and give us the power to develop a sense of self and understanding of our position within the world. Our bodies are a tremendous asset. We need to take time to celebrate them, honor them, and bring them into conscious awareness.

Even though the body holds the brain, the brain is not us. It is just a brain. Our bodies are separate from our idea of self. It is very easy to conflate the pronoun "I" with the possessive "my" when it comes to the body. Your understanding of self, your self-awareness and ego, the "I" are separate from your body, the "my." This is an important distinction to make. We are not our bodies; we just live in them. Creating that separation helps us explore our bodies' full potential, rather than treating our bodies with the same doubt we have for ourselves. If we detach our ego from our physical behavior, there is tremendous potential for expansive investigation.

The body is a powerful instrument of change.

Let's start with the notion of alignment and posture. If I ask you to stand up straight, what's the first thing you do? I will venture to guess you lifted your chest and likely tightened the muscles in the mid or lower back. You may have also held your breath and possibly clenched your jaw. Posture is not the process of posturing. Posturing is a facade. This is the unfortunate outcome of a "fake until you make it" narrative. It is us forcing our bodies to satisfy an idea of posture. Posture itself is an outcome of alignment. Posture is how your body comes to attention or gets into position to do something. It's the intricate stacking and balancing of our bones and muscles to stand up against gravity.

The way this happens effortlessly is through the power of alignment. Alignment is all about the bones, our delicious skeletal systems. Our skeletons are the building blocks for moving us through this life with ease. On their own, without muscles and tendons and connective tissue, skeletons fall into order naturally and precisely. Because we are taught to satisfy the "I" instead of the "my," to demonstrate posturing instead of posture, our muscles build habits of tension, overcompensation, or effort. Our tight muscles in our back, chest, and throat pull our skeleton out of alignment. However, if we seek posture by way of alignment, we initiate the process of "standing up straight" from the skeleton rather than from the muscle or connective tissue. Fewer muscles are engaged in the process, and as a result the entire act of "standing up straight" now feels not only easier, but more sustainable and ultimately more authentic.

Building body awareness through an objective lens, engaging in a separation from self-identity as it relates to the function of the body, is what will allow us to more effectively approach the process of developing behaviors of a confident body. Let's put this into an action context. You're sitting at a local café, reading a book, drinking a cup of coffee, when all of a sudden, your old boss walks by and notices you. He approaches your table and says with no level of irony, "Looks like you're still not into working that hard," and then walks away. Let your imagination bring a physical sensation into this reflection. The body, in circumstances like this, will follow a predictable pattern, regardless of whether you were seeking approval or think he's a jerk.

First, you will be caught off guard. Your body will translate this into a bracing of the body or an invitation for additional muscle engagement, often experienced in the form of tension. You will then experience emotional trigger and now your "I" brain is coming in hot, overriding your presence and awareness of the "my" brain, the body. Your breath is held as you try to think of something to say, but the process of holding the breath actually impairs cognitive function, so you're left simply dumbfounded and befuddled as your boss makes his way down the street.

This is the body's response to the unexpected. It is predisposed through several layers of conditioning and evolutionary patterns to move into reactive mode—fight, flight, or freeze. Through the objective observation and consistent functional practice of the behaviors of a confident body, you will, in moments like these, build habits around resilience and vulnerability that allow you to feel responsive and at ease instead of reactive, with effort.

This is probably an appropriate moment to ask, are you breathing?

I mean, I am assuming you're breathing, seeing as how you're still alive, but are you *really* breathing? Breath is the fuel for everything related to our bodies. It fuels movement, thought, and voice. The bummer is that we often limit our breath and in so doing limit our capacity for expression, presence, authenticity, and connection. Breath is an interesting function because it is automatic, it happens when we are not directing it such as while we are sleeping, and it is able to be manipulated intentionally, such as when you are feeling flustered, and you take a deep breath. Because the breath can take on identities related to your state of being, it also has to negotiate how it relates to a body that is contending with a multitude of circumstances, from simply fulfilling its most essential purpose by way of keeping you alive, all the way to arresting itself in the face of danger. The body and the breath work in unison.

There are a number of reasons why we cultivate habits around shallow breathing, most of which are brought on by stress, environmental conditions, and self-consciousness. In an article from Headspace, the renowned mediation app, Rachel Rifkin cites external factors like noise, air pollution, and temperature. She also confirms what I have seen and experienced in my work, which is cultural expectations around physical presentation, specifically flattening the belly. I know for a fact that I held my stomach in for a solid five or six years through middle school and high school thinking that it was keeping me looking trim.

What it was actually doing was creating a habit around stress. Not only is holding your belly in—which is functionally the outer abdominal wall—ineffective for deep natural breath, but it is also literally holding you in a prolonged mild stress response. If the abs are tight, the breath cannot access the lower torso and ultimately the pelvic floor. This means that the breath is now relegated to the chest, or thoracic area, which activates the sympathetic nervous system, or the fight-or-flight response. Shallow breathing means something's wrong, at least according to your body. Creating a habit of shallow breathing begins to feel like our "natural" state. We become accustomed to shallow breath and surrender all knowledge of how to welcome easy, deep breathing, which is actually our natural state.

Deep breathing is necessary, not only to reduce stress and relieve tension, but also in the process of speaking your truth.

In a study published in the National Library of Medicine, "The Effect of Diaphragmatic Breathing on Attention, Negative Affect and Stress in Healthy Adults," found that participants who were taught deep breathing exercises had reduced stress and had improved attention levels. Shallow breathing disconnects you from your body. It keeps you in a highly rational, largely cerebral space, and disconnects you from your intuitive or instinctual lower body. When the breath is able to access the pelvic floor, through deep diaphragmatic breathing, what it is really connecting to is the need to speak, our most grounded sense of self-actualization. We feel at ease and authentic.

I am not a big Chakra person, but the pelvic floor is connected to our root Chakra, which is red. I say this as a visual cue so you can land your focus there. The pelvic floor is right in the area of the perineum. If the breath moves down through the chest, into the belly with released abdominals, and makes its way to the root Chakra, you can then release on the exhale a deeply authentic vibration of impulse and intention. You are not speaking from shallow breath, which is keeping you in a state of mild anxiety. You will be speaking from a place of ease and immediacy because your body will be available to truth without fear.

I see the impact of breath directly play out in how we relate to others and our environment when I facilitate an exercise called "Eye Contact Parade." During this exercise, I ask the participants of the workshop to simply begin by walking neutrally around the room and keep their focus on themselves. Then I escalate the exercise by asking them to make eye contact with other participants as they pass them, while continuing to walk around the space. The final escalation is that when I say stop, they will pause in place, make eye contact with someone, and hold eye contact until I say go. I call it exposure therapy for eye contact.

Now, several predictable patterns emerge. One is that once the direction for the final escalation is delivered, the presence energy shifts from playful to anticipatory. The players are now in a heightened state of awareness. They slow down their walking, cautious in their movement and shallow in their breath. When I call stop and they make eye contact with someone, I allow the room to settle, wait a couple of beats, and then ask them if they are breathing. Without fail, of the dozens of times I have facilitated this exercise, there is a collective exhale almost immediately followed by a cathartic laugh of release of tension.

What this exercise demonstrates is how easy it is for us to lose connection and command of our breathing. Through the course of the exercise, I have them make eye contact several more times and hold the connection. As they become more familiar with the experience of connection (the space of vulnerability), the breath becomes less challenged and therefore the connections can become more intimate or authentic. I direct them to release their muscles and soften their gaze, to allow themselves to be seen, and to really allow themselves to see the other person. Not to just look, but really see. Sometimes this can feel too vulnerable, and we will distract ourselves by making silly faces or channeling our discomfort in self-conscious laughter.

In spite of our tremendous capacity for critical and complex thought, it is remarkable how easy it is to be undermined by the vulnerability of looking a stranger in the eyes.

When the breath stops, we hold our bodies. We also create a barrier of connection to the surrounding circumstances. The inhale and the exhale are a cycle of inspiration and expression. It is an energetic exchange. If the breath is not fueling that dynamic, it is now inorganic, disconnected from the heart, and directed by the head. The quality of expression lacks the sensation of aliveness that is what ultimately creates influence and engagement from our listener. I see this play out in public speaking. People get up in front of a large group, experience fear in their bodies, and arrest their breath in the process. This increases any present anxiety as well as assuring that an authentic connection with the audience will be impossible. The speaker is controlled and manufactured in their speech rather than immediate and intuitive. The first rule I always offer my public speaking students is "Breathe. Don't die." That always gets a laugh, but I am deadly serious. No breath, no connection to self or to others. Breath flow, body flow, brain flow, authenticity flow.

Breath is also the fuel for voice. The body, breath, and voice are the keys to a confident body, and these three functions are interdependent. The body cannot release if the breath is held. The breath cannot release if the body held. The voice cannot be free if the breath is not free. If the body is held, particularly the throat, shoulders, jaw, and chest, the voice will be strained and lack expressiveness. What's key to note here is you cannot will these functions to work effortlessly in unison. You must consciously retrain your body to come back into its most authentically natural form, meaning free in body, breath, and voice.

There is a process developed by Catherine Fitzmaurice, the originator of the Fitzmaurice Voicework®, called destructuring and restructuring. The essential methodology promotes the notion that you can destructure your habits, come back to a neutral body, free of ineffective habits, and restructure your body by intentionally introducing more effective habits. For example, if your belly is held and limiting breath capacity, you can intentionally, through a series of practices (some of which we will explore in the next section), invite the body to let go of tension in the belly and reintroduce your body to its natural state of play, expression, and connection.

Speaking should be as easy as breathing, assuming breath is flowing freely.

When we consider voice as vibration, we can now reflect on how we share our voice with others. We are no longer speaking to be heard, so much as speaking to be felt. Vibration, when produced freely, can be absorbed by your listener. A dialogue now becomes an energetic exchange rather than an execution of thoughts. Voice, when produced simply with an intention to create sound or communicate unilaterally, may be devoid of vibrancy and therefore less likely to be received as intimately or internalized as authentically by your listener. Voice is a clear indication of the health of the confident body. The characteristics and quality are symptomatic of how free the body and breath are in the transference of vibration.

Breath is fundamental to voice because the voice is carried out of the body on the breath; we call this the breath wave. Try to vocalize and hold your breath. You may get some sound, but it won't feel good or sound that great. The voice is simply a product of a well-tuned body and breath mechanism. You are actually not producing voice at all. You are producing vibration at various frequencies. Voice is what is heard by a listener. Vibration is what is produced by the speaker. In order for the listener to receive the correct notes and hear the music of your thoughts as you intend them, you have to ensure that your instrument is functioning optimally and well-tuned. If the body is distorted, it stands to reason that the sound produced from that body will also be distorted. Have you ever listened to jazz from a dented saxophone? Considering the voice as vibration places it in the realm of energy, frequency, and wavelength. The body and the breath are also composed of energy. When working harmoniously, these three elements allow for an effortless flow, inhale and exhale, of energy.

Awareness

You know that idea that once you stop looking for something you find it? Like, "Where the hell are my keys?" Then you spend thirty frantic minutes searching until you finally give up only to find them on the couch cushion next to you after you collapse in exasperation. When we are so busy looking, sometimes that prevents us from actually noticing what is around us. When you're looking hard for something, your awareness becomes hyper-focused. You put your blinders on and don't see the keys on the couch.

I'm going to call in the words of the incomparable Alan Watts for a concise insight into how we can consider the notion of exploring and observing the body in action. Watts says in his book *The Wisdom of Insecurity*, "Consciousness seems to be nature's ingenious mode of self-torture." For all his intricate philosophical prose, Watts is onto something terribly acute here. Once we become conscious to the complexities of our experience and the ego has been confronted with the ways in which we hold ourselves hostage in contention to that experience, we can't then decide we are no longer interested in knowing and bury this new knowledge below the garage.

News flash: The knowing remains. In this knowing, we only find more questions and thicker layers of uncertainty. We become conscious of our feelings about this perceived friction between us and the world. We become conscious of blaming and feeling like victims. We become conscious of our suffering and the inevitability that the suffering will continue. How, then, do we move through this world with ease and still build relationship with the world around us?

The largest challenge I have seen arise when I guide people through this work is the obstacle of objective observation. In order to access the unconscious, we must move beyond the barrier of our immediate distracted mind. For example, if I ask you to close your eyes and envision your skeleton, you may first try to think about what a skeleton looks like and draw some comparative visual reference. This may then lead your mind to think about bones and skulls. Maybe then you think about a pirate's flag and all of a sudden you are remembering a hilarious scene with Robin Williams in *Hook*, where he finally releases his imagination and sees the imaginary feast at the dinner table. Rufio!

The conscious mind is a tricky monster. It upsets our best intentions. When you consider observation, the goal is not understanding. It is not trying to know something or see something or be something. It is rather a softening of the mind and a surrendering of attachment to the layers of knowledge. The goal is not to intellectually understand your skeleton. The goal is to experience your skeleton as an integrated tool in your human experience, a part of you, distinct from the knowing self.

Observation is allowing the truth to emerge, not forcing the truth to reveal itself.

In the observation of the self, tremendous patience is required. Remember that confidence is a lifelong practice. It is not accomplished through completion of tasks, meeting of milestones, and receiving a certificate at the end. The slower you go, the faster you get there.

I was recently speaking with my incredible colleague, Patti Park. She is a lecturer and field consultant at UC Berkley, a licensed clinical social worker with a master's in social welfare and a doctorate in psychology, and a mindfulness expert. I asked her a simple, yet challenging, question. She specializes in cognitive behavioral therapy (CBT) and during a conversation about habit and behavior, I asked her, "How do we initiate the process of bringing the unconscious into conscious?"

We were approaching the notion of habit as something that we do unconsciously. It is behavior developed over time and largely without us even being aware of it. Take, for example, how you walk, the way you speak, or in more extreme cases, how you feel empowered or disempowered to express your thoughts, wants, feelings, and needs. So, if these habits are undermining our ability to live a liberated, confident life, how do we begin addressing them if we may or may not even be aware of their existence? And her response was so simple and tangible.

She said to start with the WHAT over the WHY and build a story from there. For example, when my boss calls, I stop breathing (the WHAT), which illuminates my relationship to power dynamics stemming from the relationship with my father (the WHY). Once we understand the full narrative scope of our habits and behaviors, we can then begin to recognize when they emerge and make wise decisions about how to redirect those habits. I look at this as harnessing a fact-over-feeling mindset. Carrying an objective lens of observation throughout this process will support your ability to emotionally distance yourself from the work. It becomes about the action and behavior, not about you as a person.

We develop many of these habits early on, before we are even totally self-aware, **so there is no use in feeling guilt or shame**. They are what they are. If you tend to retreat when called to rise to the occasion, that's not because you are a worthless scaredy-cat. The habit developed may be that you are holding your breath and attached to being liked rather than speaking your truth. You can now focus on releasing your breath in those moments and anchor yourself into the present, rather than allowing your behavior to be dictated by an unconscious past.

Patti identifies that your core beliefs and learned behaviors don't come out of nowhere. She takes a clearly psychological approach, but an approach that is still grounded in action and decision. She encourages her clients to not only gain clarity around their past, but also how that past operates in the present. She ultimately encourages her clients to live deeply in the momentary decision of the NOW.

She shared a story of one of her clients, with obvious respect to anonymity and doctor-patient confidentiality, who had historically experienced a lack of confidence in how she interacted with authority figures. Patti worked with her to create a story from the sequence of behaviors that surrounded the moments where she felt disempowered. The weekend before Patti and I had our conversation, this patient texted Patti to share that she had found herself in a compromising situation and, without even realizing it, was able to redirect her habit and find her voice. How incredible is that? Imagine being able to approach both the challenging and mundane moments of your life with such a deep level of agency and make powerful, instantaneous decisions. This is the foundation of mindfulness work and is the core of the work in your confidence journey. Conscious redirection of use.

At the core of confidence is presence.

Presence is a complete energetic investment in the NOW. It requires a connection to the breath, an openness of body, and a sincerity of listening. There is stillness without stiffness. There is availability to movement and expression without the habitual need to move or express. There is a seductive tension of not knowing because in deep presence there is no room for predetermination or anticipation. Imagine someone on a stage, standing still, looking out, connecting in silence, deeply present in the moment before they begin speaking. It's captivating. The moment is alive even in the absence of sound and movement. They are in the immediate and distinct landscape of the NOW. That delightful experience of "what comes next" and "how will it all end?" The practice of presence will lead to habits of presence. Layer that on with an expressive voice and playful body, and you have confidence.

Observation can also be considered as noticing. When we notice something, we are not trying to look for it. It emerges in the moment. Like our keys on the couch. You may notice someone wearing the same shirt two days in a row. You may notice a shift in your partner's tone when they say, "I love you." You may notice that you stop breathing when asking a difficult question. You cannot engage in the process of conscious redirection of use without first observing your use objectively and consciously registering what you notice.

When initiating building a practice of observation, it is worthwhile understanding the concept of practice itself. Practice is repetition. Practice will not always be driven by inspiration. Often, practice is integrated through dedicated consistency. Practice, like confidence, may encounter a threshold of resistance—that feeling of, "I really don't wanna!" Sometimes we actually don't wanna, but oftentimes we do wanna we are just avoiding practice because we are not yet at the level of proficiency and that teases our ego.

Practice in itself is a habit to be built. Much like playing piano, first you must learn where fingers go and then you learn how to move them up and down the keys with butterfly-like fluidity. The process of getting to that fluidity can be tedious and repetitive. What you need to understand most about this consistent, often uninspired dedication, is one of the most meaningful concepts I know to be true.

Practice and all is coming.

If you sit at your piano every day and fumble through scales, eventually, and often without realizing it, you are playing

Mozart. Similarly, when you practice the behaviors of confidence, you will start out feeling choppy and uncertain until all of a sudden you are playing the music of your thoughts with tremendous artistry and compelling expression.

Practice can also serve as ritual, which carries with it a sense of security and familiarity. Building the habit of practice can be challenging, as we have discussed when we addressed behavior change. The embodied practice is enlivening. It becomes a landing place for building resilience of our interiority, the space within oneself. Practice and all is coming.

Practice is about possibility rather than perfection, which shifts the engagement in the process from attachment to an ideal outcome to a direct focus and connection to the practice itself, free of constraint of idealized results. If you are seeking perfection in your practice, you will inevitably fail. Practice doesn't make perfect; it makes possible.

Perfect is a limiting belief and doesn't exist in the realm of human behavior.

On the other side of action, a public speaking moment or a moment of challenging conversation, we can feel like something went perfectly, but I guarantee if we had deliberately worked toward that exact result, the perfection would not have been attained and you would be left feeling dissatisfied once again.

What makes practice for practice sake, and trusting in the idea that if you practice all is coming, sustainable and manageable for a lifetime of implementation, is the layer of play.

This is what activates our creativity, alleviates the consequence of messing up, and brings presence to the process of practice. Play is the ingredient of surrender. When we practice, failure is inevitable. In life, failure is inevitable. By harnessing the habit of play, you will experience failure as the gift of new information rather than a reflection of your ultimate capability.

Let's think about play very deliberately. Play is not un-serious. It is not a frivolous action in service of a ridiculous outcome, with an expectation of laughter, and maybe a clown or some funny voices. Play is not mindless. It is incredibly mindful and deeply intentional. Play is strategic decision-making. Play is creative and innovative thinking. Play is imagination come alive. Play is listening and responding. Play is a full commitment. Play is a willingness to look silly or foolish in service of something greater than yourself. Play is hypothesis in action.

Think about the action and behavior of a person you perceive as confident; you will notice a balance of trust in their command of the moment and an equally present tension of the unpredictable. That is the landscape of play. Play allows you to work alongside your ego, rather than let it always call the shots. Play is what allows you to observe, notice, and respond freely.

Play is the most powerful tool in the toolkit of human behavior.

We have largely forgotten how to play (initiate emotional symphonic underscore), and as a result we have lost connection with what it means to be human.

The next time you are feeling curious, defensive, or at odds with your circumstances, I want you to ask yourself one simple question, "I wonder what would happen if...." That's all it takes to ignite play, bring you into an observant present, and allow the habit of practice to feel a bit more inspired. You have dedicated your presence to these pages and prepared yourself to surrender to the practices of a confident body. The coming chapters will move you into kinesthetic practice. We will turn theory into functional exploration. Stay present, stay patient, stay playful.

PLAY

Directing the Body

I remember when I was first learning to drive. The process began long before I got behind the wheel. I would watch my mom drive on the way home from school. I watched how she turned the wheel and slowed the car as we entered a sharp turn on the back country roads, and then observed her right the wheel and accelerate as we came out of the turn. I watched cars whiz by right outside of her window on these narrow passages, and my mother, like some stoic superhero, was completely unfazed.

I remember when I finally got behind the wheel myself. With a teenage heart full of hubris, I assumed I'd be great at it on the first try. I had already learned to drive a tractor and a riding lawn mower, after all. We started training in the classic manner of an empty school parking lot. I got behind the wheel of our Dodge Minivan, and all of a sudden, my hand eye coordination went completely out the window. I couldn't look at the road and the speedometer and my rearview mirror at the same time. My eyes were frantically darting around, my breath was locked in my chest, my hands lost their grip on the wheel. It was bananas! Did people really do this?

I moved slowly at first, feeling the resistance of the gas pedal under my foot. I could feel the transmission shift into second gear and produce a slight burst of acceleration. Negotiating between steering and pushing the pedals was a full-on "pat head, rub belly" situation. It was a delicate process of cautious anticipation. Eventually I felt in command enough that my mother felt okay to take me out on the open road.

About a mile into my adventure, there was a stop sign. I came to a complete stop and dutifully looked both ways before proceeding. I made my way down a rolling hill, turkey and sheep farms on either side. I was approaching the turn to go back to our house, and I guess I was feeling very confident at this point, having now been an official driver for all of thirty minutes, that I made the move for a quick left turn as if I had been personally driving this route for years.

What I failed to anticipate was the small hill coming toward us that would hide any oncoming cars until the last moment. As I went to turn, a car emerged right at the crest of the little hill, about forty feet away, with full intention of going straight ahead, unencumbered by the likes of a novice driver like myself. I had just moved to initiate the turn and was now caught off guard while driving a vehicle at twenty-five miles an hour. I decided to just go for the turn and zip in front of this other car. Simultaneously, my mother is in full panic mode and tells me to stop because the other car has the right of way. So, I stop...in the middle of the road, blocking the other car. My mother tells me, "Just keep going and pull over there!" Thus, ending my first driving lesson. I am happy to report that I finally got the hang of things and have maintained an excellent driving record. Except for the one incident when I hit a cow, but that's a story for another day.

Learning to observe the self, redirect the behaviors of the self, and embody those behaviors to the point of habit is a lot like learning to drive. You begin by observing confidence in people around you. Then you begin to perceive yourself as capable of embodying similar behavior. Eventually, you begin to explore and practice those behaviors to bring them into habit. One plus one equals two.

The initial part of the process will feel clunky and unrefined. It might be experienced as labored or lacking finesse. This is a necessary part of the process of developing behaviors of confidence. At a certain point, these clunky new actions and behaviors become embodied behaviors and moved into habit, thus becoming your "natural" state. Like driving, at some point you just need to hit the open road, stay sharp, and hope for the best. But first, you have to start in the parking lot.

In the process of directing the body, you cannot expect new habits or behaviors to become integrated during day-to-day activity and interactions.

Practice must happen separately from real life, with intentional space created for observation and redirection. The reason for this is because our unconscious behavior habits will override our desired new habits within familiar or routine circumstances. When I work with clients on speech and accent reduction, they will never experience a shift in habits of articulation if they are only working toward it in conversation. Their historical habits will win every time. Speech practice, like any new practice, must happen separately and in a dedicated, intentional way.

Moving from observation into redirection will feel challenging initially, perhaps almost like slow motion. The process goes: observe use, intervene on old habits, redirect toward new habits, execute redirection. For example, I hold my breath when I brush my teeth, I direct myself to release my belly and free my breath as I brush my teeth, I bring conscious awareness to my breath every time I reach for my toothbrush.

Integrating the practice of redirection should always begin in low-stakes situations, like a weekly phone call with your mom or when speaking to your kids. In these interactions, the risk of failure or judgment is lower, and therefore, you will feel more open to taking the risk. Ultimately, the ability to redirect yourself will become second nature. You will realize you're holding your breath as you reach for your toothbrush. You will redirect your body to release the breath into the belly and lower the amount of tension present during such a routine activity. How you do anything is how you do everything.

The practice of redirection will move from a slow motion, multi-step, hyper-conscious process, into one that is deeply embodied.

The practice of redirection becomes habit itself, and the time it takes to consciously redirect the body will be nearly instantaneous and deeply intuitive. For example, once you learn to drive and are very good at it, it is much easier to adapt to things like potholes or sharp turns. The more you practice, the easier it is to integrate changes that ultimately get you where you want to go. At that point, you will be ready to bring the practice of redirection into higher stakes scenarios and implement this conscious and intuitive awareness in a strategic way. I like to think about this as learning to play the instrument of your body.

Let's examine how conscious redirection operates in real-life and high-performance moments. We will examine three distinct examples. I will first describe the scenario. I will then walk you through what you may generally experience in the moments when you are called to rise to the occasion or unexpectedly called to action. Last, I will break down the redirection into micro actions. Keep in mind, the redirection of micro actions takes about as long as a thought in practice but will take a bit longer in the explanation. It's like watching a moment in film. You can break it down frame by frame, but when sped up it lasts only as long as the blink of an eye.

All examples take place in person but assume similar principles of redirection apply for virtual interaction.

PUBLIC SPEAKING
Max is an expert on fundraising. He has a desire to establish himself as a thought leader in addition to his consulting work with nonprofits. Max is invited to speak to a group of executive directors of various nonprofits on the mindset and embodiment of abundance as it relates to fundraising. This speaking opportunity will take place in person to an

audience of approximately 300 people. Max will be wearing a lavalier mic, allowing his hands to be free.

Max is at the venue, standing in the wings of the stage, awaiting his keynote introduction. He looks out at the audience and is confronted with the scale of the crowd. Max is hit with a wave of adrenaline. There is energy coursing through his body. He is rapidly repeating moments of his talk that he always forgets. He wants to make sure he is remembering the important moments. Because his body is prioritizing his adrenaline, his attempt to "remember" anything is unsuccessful. The person introducing Max finally completes their welcome and calls Max to the stage.

Max has a habit of starting as soon as his name is called or when someone says "go." This time is no different. He skips over the moment of connecting intentionally and authentically with the audience, even though he offers a warm hello. He skips ahead of the moment of readiness and begins before he is ready. It's like a track runner setting off in a sprint before the starting shot is fired. His head and his heart spend the first few moments trying to sync up with one another. He remembers his speech, thank goodness, but the initial minutes of the speech are delivered as recitation rather than with a desire to be heard. He is trying to remember, rather than trusting his memory. He is speaking at his audience instead of to his audience. Vocally he is loud, but he lacks resonance and sounds monotone. His breath is tight because his hips are tight, and he is disconnected from his lower body. He is ungrounded.

Here's how Max can consciously direct himself to rise to the occasion of a keynote address:

The moment Max is called on stage, he directs himself to breathe and feel his feet. As Max walks across the stage toward the center, he consciously tracks two points of focus—the person who welcomed him and the audience. This will likely create an impulse to over-perform or to move out of authenticity. This happens because as he enters from behind the wings, he enters into an awareness of being seen. His ego kicks in and wants to protect itself from flaw and failure. The body tenses. He is prepared for his body to respond this way and directs himself to release his shoulders and breathe.

In this moment, Max consciously feels his feet as he makes his way across the stage. Instead of scanning the room, he intentionally lands his focus on one or two spots in the audience, maybe even making eye contact if possible. He directs himself to breathe and releases his shoulders. As he approaches the person who welcomed him, he genuinely meets that person, sees them, and exchanges places deliberately. He now becomes the focus for the audience.

There is an energetic calibration that has to happen here. He consciously registers this need to calibrate and increase the relationship between himself and the audience. This all happens in the matter of moments. Max observes his nervousness showing up as a little voice inside him telling him "not to mess up." He consciously directs his awareness toward the audience, thereby interrupting the spiral down the dark chasm of self-defeat. He is there to offer something, not be judged on his performance. Max settles his body and directs himself to begin with intention and when he is ready. Max is now in a state of presence, having surrendered to the impossibility of perfection as part of his daily practice toward confident behavior.

As Max is moving through his content, he gets to one of the places where he is uncertain about the key points and what comes next. This pulls him into his head and away from connecting with the audience. He is no longer focused on delivering, but rather on remembering. Because his intention has shifted, his connection to intentional expression is lost. He starts to pace around the room, in passive presentation instead of active presentation. The audience disengages from him. He is no longer demanding their participation, and he can feel them floating away. Max becomes aware that he has moved into his head and is wandering around the stage without great specificity.

Max directs himself to pause and visually land his focus outside of himself. On the next thought, he moves to a deliberate point on the stage and stops to deliver the thought in place. This allows him to not only physically punctuate the thought and create a visual guide of the flow of thought for the audience, but it also allows Max to regain command over the execution of his thoughts in action.

By directing himself to land his body in certain zones—we will call them blocking zones—he still gives himself the opportunity to move without inviting extraneous movement. When he gets to a natural pause or shift in thought, he uses that as a cue to breathe and move to a new zone. Breath fuels movement. He remembers to release the muscles of his face and drop his shoulders. As he moves to a new zone, he consciously registers the attentiveness of the audience and, when he arrives at the new zone, continues with his talk, having regained connection to the listener. Even though Max had a few hiccups, by redirecting his body, he was able to stay authentic and effectively communicate his ideas in his speech.

MEETING NEW PEOPLE

Elsie is an engineer. She has a graduate degree and has been working professionally in the architecture space for three years. She is relatively new to her field but was fortunate to get recruited by a top firm. She was furloughed at the start of the pandemic quarantine and was ultimately let go. Elsie has been hunting for a job for eight months. As a component of her job seeking journey, she has started to deliberately network. Elsie sometimes struggles during social events that are crowded or loud. She enjoys talking to people, but meeting them for the first time makes her a bit anxious. She has felt more comfortable networking virtually because she can be in greater control of her environment and circumstances. She has been invited to attend an in-person networking event and reluctantly agrees because her ideal employer will be represented there.

Elsie has just entered the location of the networking event. It is during the evening at a local bar's pack patio. She walks through the bar toward the back. She hears the sound of people talking and starts to physically hold her body as she is struck with a physical sensation of anticipation. Her mind starts to send signals to abort the mission. Turn around and go home. She rounds her shoulders slightly forward and dips her chin in a diminishing posture as she forges ahead and makes her way to the back patio. She gets there, and the crowd is fairly large.

She becomes aware of people's faces and their glances in her direction. She is unsure where to look. She is holding her breath as she scans the space, looking for the person who invited her. As she is looking around, someone approaches to introduce themselves. She is caught off guard. Her body freezes and she becomes aware of her hands caught between shaking and not shaking the person's hand. The person who approached her, smiles, and says hello, followed by a short introduction. Elsie is not making present eye contact. She is not sure where to look.

This lack of visual focus causes her mind to become less anchored on listening. She does not register the person's name or personal details. The person then asks her name. She finally looks the person in the eye, her shoulders still curved in a submissive posture, and says her name is Elsie and she is currently on the job search. The person says, "Well, you came to the right place." Elsie doesn't respond. The person then asks where she worked previously. Elsie responds with just the name of the firm, but no further details. The person, fortunately, recognizes the firm and has a couple of colleagues who work there. Again, Elsie says nothing, but nods this time. The person finally surrenders, wishes her a good time, and moves on to another conversation.

Here's how Elsie can redirect herself to achieve a more authentic first impression and open the door to a more fluid conversation:

Elsie is walking into the bar where the event is being held. Before she even enters, she takes a moment outside to shake out her face and connect to her breath. She establishes a clear intention for the evening, which is to learn about what it's like to work for this ideal employer. Elsie makes her way to the back patio. As she approaches, she hears talking and lots of conversations. She starts to feel resistance in her body. She is familiar with this physical sensation. She directs her body to soften, releasing through the shoulders and the butt. She shakes out her hands and continues outside. She takes a moment to receive the space before beginning to look for her colleague. She takes it in as an objective observer and remembers to breathe.

As she is receiving the space, she is approached by a person she does not know. She has a moment of surprise and immediately brings her face alive with a smile, to convey welcome as well as initiate the breath and lead to easier vocalization. The person extends their hand, and she goes for a fist bump. Instead of allowing this misalignment in preferred post-COVID salutation to undermine her presence, she instead laughs and verbally acknowledges her confusion about what is appropriate. This creates immediate familiarity.

Names are exchanged along with general introduction details, all while Elsie is intentionally directing her focus toward active listening. She is making occasional direct eye contact, allowing her gaze to shift, but always keeping the focus outside of herself. She continues to be conscious of her breath. The person then shares that they have colleagues who work at her old company. Instead of freezing and not responding, Elsie consciously responds with a "yes, and" framework.

The key components of this tool are 1) acknowledge, 2) elevate, 3) advance. She is able to insert three simple phrases to move the conversation forward, while staying on topic and accepting what the other person said. "(1) Yes, there are such incredible people who work there (2) AND I am impressed by your familiarity with the firm. (3) Quality in people is just as important as quality of the product." She is able to continue the conversation because she is not focused internally on what she should say next, but rather maintaining external focus, listening deeply, and responding with "yes, and."

We are all capable of living in a confident body.

In these two examples, there are endless directions you could offer because your body, the history of your use, the habits of your behavior, will have utterly unique manifestations. Maybe your leg starts to shake when you get nervous. Maybe you have a tendency to speak loudly to compensate for fear and become tight in the lower back. Maybe you become stiff in your movement, tight in the armpits, and confused in the mind. The primary thing to recognize is that you are consistently at choice and have abundant agency about how you are playing the instrument of your body. You can always be present to your breath, your focus, and the freedom or constraint of the voice. You can direct yourself to listen. You can take time to center yourself before you engage in a situation that seems intimidating. You can consciously implement tools to support your communication and maintain your presence. You may have a different way in which these three scenarios play out, but you will have the same number of options for how to be in conscious use and deeply present in your body.

I remember one Equity (the stage actors' union) audition I went on in NYC. It was for a tour of a Shakespeare play. I had just graduated with my MFA in acting and had done my thesis performance as Prospero in *The Tempest,* so I was feeling pretty self-assured about how the audition would go. I was waiting outside of the audition room, and my focus was entirely misdirected. I was not grounding myself or getting in my body and preparing it to effectively deliver my monologue. Instead, I was scanning the waiting area and assessing the others present. I was a new Equity member and was feeling a bit intimidated by other, more seasoned, actors also auditioning. I was listening in on conversations happening about what auditions were coming up, what shows were going to open soon, whose agent had sent them out for which audition. I had this distinct feeling of being out of my league. But, as was typical of my behavior, I ignored those feelings of insecurity and continued to distract my mind with arrogant comparison.

The audition coordinator came into the waiting area and called for Minna Taylor. I was abruptly pulled out of my eavesdropping and called to attention that it was my turn to present my audition. I was scattered in the collection of my belongings and, in a rush, followed the coordinator into the audition room. The room was much larger than I had anticipated, and I felt more seen than felt comfortable. The director and casting director were sitting at a folding table at the far end of the room, so I had to walk all the way across, plastering an enthusiastic smile on my face, to deliver my headshot and resume to them. I was not breathing. They were very friendly and welcomed me in, invited me to place my belongings on the chair near them, and asked me what monologue I would be presenting. I believe it was a piece from *Measure for Measure*, but I honestly can't remember.

I was not as prepared as I could have been in terms of familiarity with the monologue and didn't give myself adequate time to get present. I was conscious of them observing me as I walked to the center of the room to present my piece, and this totally distracted me from centering myself in the space. My focus was on what they were thinking rather than preparing for what I was about to do. I landed in place and moved directly into executing the text. I didn't calibrate myself in terms of where I was going to land my focus or allow my body to prepare to engage in the defined objective. I simply began before I was ready. Almost immediately, my leg started to shake. Not a tapping of the foot or a mild tremor, but a full-on undulation of nervousness. My right knee was bucking to the right, and I could not plant my heel for the life of me. I was aware of this happening, but rather than pause and breathe, I trudged through and completed the piece with tremendous effort.

The director and casting director looked befuddled but couldn't have been more gracious as they wished me well on the rest of my day. I walked the long walk back to the door, feeling a film of regret encase me as I turned the knob to exit.

Here's how I could have empowered myself to rock that freaking audition (even if that didn't mean I was the one they ultimately cast):

In the waiting area, instead of distracting myself with self-conscious eavesdropping, I am intentional about connecting to my breath and grounding myself in the objective of the monologue. I review the text once out loud and think through the important moments of the character. I am aware that my turn to audition is coming up, so I am prepared to not only deliver the text, but to engage with the casting table. My name is called by the coordinator, but I am not caught off guard. I am ready to transition into performance mode.

I enter the room and take it in with a breath as I acknowledge the director and casting director at the far side. I walk over, connecting with them the entire way with presence, free of urgency. I hand them my headshot and resume, set down my belongings, and walk to the middle of the room. As I am walking, I am centering myself back into my body in order to connect to the objective of the monologue. I take a moment to identify where I will be looking to deliver the monologue (typically a spot on the wall above the casting director, not directly at the casting director). I take a breath, feel my feet, and begin when I am ready. I move through the text with a couple of moments of uncertainty; however, when they arise, I intentionally pause and redirect my attention toward my connection to my why or objective rather than my delivery or performance. My voice is free, and my body is at ease but still engaged.

I complete the monologue, allow for a moment of settling and transition, and land my focus back on the casting table to say thank you. They thank me for the audition; I collect my belongings, and I exit the door feeling complete in my performance and present in my body.

So...

What was experienced in the first examples is indicative of what happens when we lose present awareness of self. When we become distracted by our ego and disconnected from our breath. By landing attention back on our bodies, our physical use, and relationship to our circumstances that were in our control, we were able to make wise decisions about how to negotiate challenging moments when we were called to rise to the occasion. One plus one equals two.

Movement and Vibration

When it comes to the romantic notions we hold about the majesty of human behavior, we rarely think about it from a functional perspective, nor should we. We don't watch a captivating speech from a beloved public icon and think, "Wow, they were really in their feet and connected to their breath." This romantic image of a confident person, the inspiration or intimacy we may experience, is the lens of the outside observer, the witnessing body. The perceiver of confidence. What we are experiencing as an audience is not the functionality of confidence, but rather the authentic and honest expression of that functionality. This seemingly intangible essence of confidence is functionally developed through habits of movement and vocalization without rigid boundary and existing in the distinct landscape of the unknown. This is the functional action of play and presence.

Keith Johnstone, author of *Impro: Improvisation and the Theatre* and one of the foremost authorities on improvisation, shares, "In cases of extreme stage fright, the space is like a plastic skin pressing on to you and making your body rigid and bound. The opposite of this is seen when a great actor makes a gesture, and it's as if his arm has swept right over the heads of the people sitting at the back of the audience." (Johnstone, 1979) When our bodies react to fear, the breath becomes shallow and the body responds with tension. The voice becomes restricted and loses vibrancy. It feels like there is a restrictive boundary around us and we cannot break the barrier. The image of an actor gesturing all the way to the back of the audience implies a complete release of the body, openness of breath, and freedom of expression. This does not mean a body is out of control of intention and rational guidance through the observant mind. Instead, it is an integrated marriage of impulse and intention. It is the ultimate expression of authentic behavior and truth telling in action.

One of the biggest barriers I have witnessed in my clients is in the process of moving beyond their physical habit and comfort zone of expression and the risk of looking foolish doing it. Taking on technical direction is much easier. When I walk them through tools for confident public speaking, the first access point, or level one public speaking, is the "what to do with my hands and where do I take a pause" section. This will get them through the fundamentals of how to engage with material in front of an audience. The outcome is usually pretty boring and stiff, but they get through it. Level two public speaking is more challenging to implement. This is where you allow presence and play to bring your humanity to public speaking. The body, however, must be prepared to rise to this occasion. That's where playful practice comes in.

I will challenge my clients to use their voices in playful ways, moving beyond their habitual vocal patterns. They will, almost without fail, increase volume and the use of the facial muscles, but neglect to actually shift the tone, pitch, or resonance of their voice. They are too in control, held too tightly to the outcome or intended result. They are focused on how the voice sounds versus how the voice feels.

There is tremendous challenge, for example, altering the pattern of upspeak (using a questioning tone at the end of a statement). This is not because the muscles are resistant or incapable, but because the habit is so ingrained and unconscious that even identifying where the upspeak takes place can be a challenge. The speaker becomes immune to it. They will repeat a phrase over and over, attempting to incorporate the direction to shift their voice downward at the end of a thought, and be unable to move the voice or engage the redirection.

It is hard to shift habits around free and dynamic expression of the voice and body without going big and very deliberately moving far outside the boundary of the comfort zone. This is the role of play.

In the theater, we use a technique called an Italian Run to bring new life to a play once all the technical aspects of the play have been established. In order to shake up habits, patterns, and predictability (which is the death of live theater), we rehearse the play quickly, with exaggerated movements and almost caricature-like vocal production, while still holding on to the truth of our intention. This level of play is such a vital piece of building confidence. The aliveness found in presence, the immediacy, the unknown, is the layer required to captivate an audience and elevate the performer into behaviors of confidence. If the play were rehearsed with the goal of simply putting on a technically correct performance, there would be no art. There would only be actors reciting lines, manufacturing moments of connection, and moving around the stage mechanically. The Italian Run concept allows the actors to move into presence, upset the expected, stay within what is rehearsed while amplifying its expression. This brings aliveness. This is what the audience pays to see.

Adding on to your practices of observation and redirection, you can now incorporate the practice of play. This practice will catapult you into presence by default. We will explore this in the voice, body, and gesture. You will feel silly. You may experience resistance to engaging the body and voice in purposeless ways that are juvenile or childlike. Observe this experience in your body. We will start simply and increase the play and expanse of expression incrementally. I will inch you toward the edge of the cliff, the precipice of truth, and talk you through how to take the leap across to the land of possibility. Your full potential awaits you there.

The series of exercises I will outline are organized in a way that allows you to ground yourself in your body and come into presence. You will connect with the breath and feel the deepening of the breath in stillness. You will then activate simple and routine movement. Following movement, you will activate vibration for the simple experience or feeling the vibration, but no attention to the produced sound or volume will be given at this point. This step is for you to understand the simple experience of freely releasing vibration. Speaking should be as easy as breathing. Confidence should be as easy as breathing in the moment. At each interval, stay present to the observation of the body and breath at a functional level. Where are you experiencing resistance? Use the exaggeration of vibration and energy expression of your body and voice to break through the resistance. Get playful.

BREATH AND MOVEMENT
Stillness is a powerful tool for presence and authenticity. Nothing can be hidden in stillness. So much can be witnessed and perceived. If stillness is present, free from stiffness or tension, movement and the availability for expression will exist. This is the electric space of the moment before. Esther Perel, world renowned psychotherapist and author of the book *Mating in Captivity*, refers to this as the space of erotic intelligence. (Perel, 2006) The space where anything can happen and simultaneously nothing needs to happen. It activates. It titillates and inspires. It intimidates. It intoxicates.

Stillness with presence is the most powerful posture one can assume.

EXERCISE → STILLNESS AND ALIGNMENT
Stand with your feet on the floor, hip width apart, and parallel. You want to align your feet to the skeleton hips or hip creases, rather than the outer edge of the rounded, fleshy hip. This will likely feel as though your feet are too close together, as many of us are conditioned toward a wider, more dominant stance. Placing your feet under your hips is more structurally sound and will require less effort from the rest

of your body, while allowing you to feel grounded in effortless activation.

1. Observe how your feet make contact with the floor. Imagine they create a rectangle on the floor. Are all four corners making contact with the floor or are you favoring the front, back, or sides of the feet? This will serve as a foundation for easy alignment.

2. Close the eyes. Take a moment to quiet the mind and bring your attention into yourself. Come into presence with this moment.

3. Breathe through the mouth. This will feel strange, and you will have to remind yourself continuously to breathe through the mouth during this section of the practice. If this is challenging to maintain, place the tip of your tongue outside of the mouth on the lower lip. This will open up the throat and maintain effortless breathing.

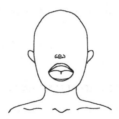

4. Consciously observe the body in space and walk your awareness through a full-body check-in for tension and ineffective use. Implement the practice of redirection toward softening and releasing. What can you do less

of? Starting with the feet, the knees, the thighs, the hips, the belly, the butt, the lower back, the chest, the armpits, the hands, the shoulder blades, the back of the neck, the front of the throat, the tongue, the forehead, the jaw. You will likely be negotiating between relaxed and released, wanting to collapse in the spine or stiffen up. This is natural and an opportunity for curiosity and observation.

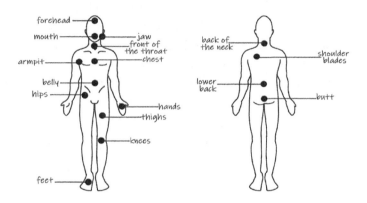

5. The body knows how to breathe itself. Inhale and exhale. When the body inspires, it receives inspiration. When it expires, it expresses itself. Inhale to inspire. Exhale to express. Allow the body to live in its natural breath rhythm. Observe where the body is resisting the breath through tension. Release.

6. Bring your attention to the spine. Your spine is a vertical alignment of vertebrae and cartilage. With your eyes still closed, imagine your spine along your back. Keep breathing. Feel the spine extending toward the base of the skull and grounding through the sacrum, or pelvis

area. The spine is the catalyst for movement. It is the axis of effortlessness.

7. Visualize the breath on the inhale, traveling down the spine, all the way down to the pelvic floor. On the exhale, visualize the breath spiraling up the spine, maintaining effortless activation of length and alignment.

8. On an exhale, drop your chin toward your chest. Just your chin. Do your best not to control this movement. Simply release the muscles on the back of the neck as you exhale. Feel the weight of your head bring a passive stretch to the shoulders as it hangs forward with gravity.

9. Allow the weight of your head, leading with the crown of the skull, to guide your spine into inverted length, one vertebra at a time. Visualize the spine rolling down, slowly on the breath. Visualizing space being introduced between each vertebra.

10. Feel the breath move into the belly and into the back space. You will feel the soft tissue between the ribs, the intercostals, expand as you roll through the spine. You will feel them expand and contract naturally with each cycle of inhale and exhale.

11. Bend the knees slightly as you find your way to a fully rolled down position. Feel the breath deeply in the lower body, expanding the glutes and softening the hips.

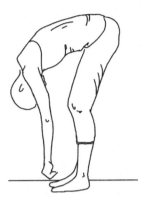

12. Hang in the rolled over position and allow gravity to pull you into effortless inverted alignment. Breathe through the mouth. Sway your torso from side to side. Notice if the feet are still creating a strong foundation. Release the shoulders and arms.

13. Initiating from the base of the spine, you will now slowly direct your body toward a standing posture by visualizing the spine restacking each vertebra, one on top of the other, while maintaining the space between each vertebra that was introduced while rolling down.

14. Back in standing, in stillness, check-in with the full body. Starting with the feet and moving all the way to the jaw. Breathe through the mouth.

15. Gently repeat the process.

You are now in stillness, a grounded posture of readiness. Open your eyes and see the environment around you. How are you existing in the space after connecting to your body and breath? You have now become the watcher or observer of your experience and placed yourself in a space ready to respond versus react.

Cultivating the posture of stillness is like creating a blank canvas for truth telling. From this space, you can layer on your intention, your gesture, and your movement in precise and unexpected ways. To allow the body to be available to expressive and dynamic movement, you must guide your body into the habit of movement free of tension.

As you incorporate various muscles and activations into the practice, your body will begin to revert to habits of control and tension. Be present to this inevitability with an objective redirecting mind. Notice, as you shift from stillness into movement, how your body responds and where you can grant it permission to do less, in service of allowing for more.

EXERCISE → MOVEMENT
Before you set to move, integrate the direction of thinking to move.

The thought of movement, similar to initiating vocalization, will trigger preparatory habits. This may look like a tensing of the back of the neck when you go to take a step or tightening the belly as you go to shake someone's hand. This is your opportunity to intervene and consciously redirect toward optimal function of use.

1. Find yourself in a neutral standing posture. Feel your feet below you and bring your attention to the alignment and stability of your skeleton.

2. Initiate a full-body check-in as outlined in step 4 of the stillness section. Remember to breathe.

3. Think about the moment of transitioning from stillness into movement, rather than the movement itself. Walking is something we have built tremendous habit around and will be quite easy to fall out of presence with. Do not take for granted that you know what you're doing. There is a lot going on to which you are entirely unconscious. Stay diligent.

4. Bring your attention to the right foot. From the heel to the toes, roll through your foot gently. Feel the movement of all the muscles and soft tissue between the bones of the foot. Feel the roll motion make its way through the tip of your big toe. Reset your foot on the floor. Repeat this process with your left foot. Notice how your body compensates for balance as you simply and effortlessly explore the undulation of your feet. Keep breathing.

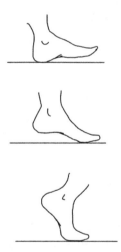

5. Back in a neutral posture, roll through your right foot, allowing it to come off the floor, and leverage the momentum to bring your right knee in front of your body. Be mindful to release the hips and allow the lower abdomen to mildly engage in service of lifting the leg. Gently place the foot back down beneath you. Repeat this process with your left foot and knee.

6. Observe how your breath reacts to this increase in exertion. Observe what muscles engage and identify how you can consciously redirect unnecessary engagement toward release. Pro tip: Your upper body and head are not involved in the practice of rolling through the foot. Have you invited them to the party by accident?

7. Repeat the process of rolling through the right foot, lifting the knee, and now place the foot in front of you as if you are taking a step. Do this movement slowly and mindfully. This will require balance but should not be too challenging if you are doing it slowly enough to calibrate balance and redirect preparatory or compensatory habits in the process. You will notice that your left foot will naturally rise in the heel and shift the weight toward the ball of the foot as your body weight shifts back over both feet. Your right foot should be fully grounded.

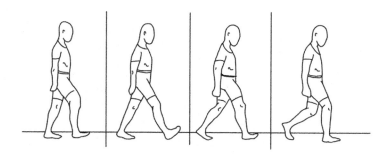

8. Repeat this process immediately on the left side, allowing you to take two full steps. Do this mindfully and with conscious movement.

9. Your upper body is neutral. You do not need your chin, your hands, your shoulder, etc. to do anything in service of moving your body through space. This exercise is building information around how your body invites, initiates, and propels movement.

10. Take several conscious steps around the room by following the steps of roll through the foot, lift the knee, place the foot in front of you, repeat. Breathe.

11. Observe your gaze as you consciously walk through the space. Keep it lifted. You do not need to look down. Keep your gaze straight on the horizon.

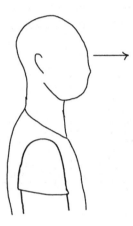

This entire practice will probably feel very mechanical. That is exactly where you should be. The function precedes the freedom.

EXERCISE → VIBRATION

As we have noted, voice is what you hear, and vibration is what you create. When you engage in the process of vocalization, the lens you want to activate as a method for conscious redirection is the feeling of your voice rather than the sound of your voice. The distinct reasoning here is that focusing on the sound places your attention on the outcome rather than the process itself. Staying present to the experience of vibration allows you to stay present to the action of communication as a holistic process and offers you the opportunity to strategically shift vibration depending on the nature and needs of any given interaction.

Your body is an instrument. The above exercises will tune your body to play the notes you intend with intention, clarity, and availability for improvisation. Building a habit of effortless vocalization will allow your audience to fully receive your message. A vibrant voice can penetrate your listener. A voice focused on volume will confront your listener.

We are speaking to be felt.

1. Gather several coffee table books that you will feel comfortable placing on your belly and set them by your side.

2. Begin lying on the floor. Your feet will be on the floor and your knees will be bent. You may want to place a small item (a folded hand towel or thing book) under your head to support your neck. Allow your hands to fall to the side, close your eyes, and breathe through the mouth.

3. Allow yourself to come back into presence after you have transitioned into this position. Your body will likely brace itself against the floor by arching in the lower back, clenching the butt, tightening the belly, or holding up the neck and shoulders. Consciously redirect your body to release and surrender to gravity. Sink in.

4. Eyes closed, breathing through the mouth, simply take ten breaths here. Inhale, exhale with no added effort in terms of depth of inhale or energy of exhale. Be mindful to release the lips and soften the tongue. Observe your mind wandering and the body's continuous desire to over-engage in a fully relaxed position.

5. After the ten breaths, very gently, with as little effort as possible, grab your coffee table books and place them on the lower belly. Your body will again brace itself against this added weight. Allow for the recalibration process to happen. Sink in.

6. With the books on your belly, take ten more breaths through the mouth. Nice and easy. Your body knows how to breathe itself, even with a stack of coffee table books on your belly. You don't need to do anything additional beyond observing your body and breath.

7. After ten breaths, with as little effort as possible, remove the books from the belly and place them at your side. Take ten more breaths here, feeling the breath now redirected toward the lower body. Observe the openness of the hips and the release of the outer abdominals.

8. Bring your hands to your belly, inhibiting any ineffective use or unnecessary engagement of the shoulders or neck. Using your fingertips, start to pulse the belly. This is called a belly shakeout. You will likely feel resistance at first because your belly is attempting to protect itself. It's like what happens when someone tickles you. That is totally natural. Invite your body to release anywhere that is not in use. As you pulse your belly, allow the breath to be audible. Breathing through the mouth, releasing the lips. Place your tongue on your lower lip if this feels challenging.

9. On the exhale, *think* about creating vibration on a haaaa sound. Do not move to create vibration yet. Observe how your body prepares to "speak." What muscles come into play that are unnecessary? Speaking should be as easy as breathing. How can you make it easier? Release the throat, soften the belly, release the middle back, release the neck.

10. On the exhale, initiate vibration while pulsing the belly as the breath is being carried out of the mouth. This may feel challenging from such a relaxed position. Have no expectation for volume. Vibration is fueled by breath. Feel the moment when vibration is created in the larynx or voice box. Feel the vibration fill the chest cavity and enter into the mouth. Feel how the vibration fills the skull. Feel the vibration exit the mouth on the breath. Allow the vibration to come to completion outside of the mouth.

11. Repeat this as many times as you please. You can play around with moving the vibration up and down in pitch.

12. To begin exploring the strength of tone, practice landing your vibration on the ceiling above you. Observe how your body responds to this elevated activation and intentional amplification. What can you do less of? How can you allow for greater vibration through a conscious release of tension and ineffective habit?

13. Release the pulsing motion and place one hand on your chest, allowing the other arm to fall gently to the side. Initiate vibration from this simple place and feel the vibration in your chest with your hand. You will experience stronger vibration when the voice is fully released. How can you do less to allow for more?

PASS THE SOUND AND GESTURE (TO BE PLAYED WITH FRIENDS!)
This exercise is ideal for demonstrating the inherent individuality in how we interact and approach the same things differently. The exercise celebrates this notion and encourages full expression of your interpretation of the sound and gesture. Think about it like a physical telephone. This game also necessitates listening and communicating intentionally. A distinct lens should be placed on how you prepare or anticipate receiving the sound and gesture and how committed and present you are in passing the sound and gesture. It is the perfect exercise to evaluate your willingness to lean into the

silly, to embrace the foolish, and to gain information around how you advance or retreat in the moment when called to rise to the occasion.

1. In a group of at least four people (I have conducted this exercise with over seventy people!), stand in a circle with about an arm's length between each person.

2. One person volunteers to start the game. (I will often ask for a volunteer before explaining the exercise, so as to not discourage participation and risk taking.)

3. The volunteer will deliver their sound and gesture to the person to the right or left of them. The starting direction doesn't matter. Clockwise or counterclockwise are both perfectly fine.

4. The gesture can be whatever they like but must be accompanied by a sound. For example, I throw my arms in the air and caw like a crow or I snap my fingers and shuffle my feet as I make the sound of a snare drum played with brushes (che-che-che). The only requirement is that they fully commit vocally and physically.

5. The person to whom they pass their sound and gesture, receives the communication, turns to the person on the other side of them, and delivers the sound and gesture. This continues until the sound and gesture have been passed all the way around the circle. Again, it's like a physical telephone.

6. Common challenges that arise are the impact of anticipation on presence and the impact of vulnerability around using their body and voice in unusual and likely ridiculous ways.

7. Ask for a new volunteer to initiate a new sound and gesture and repeat the exercise.

Key considerations for group reflection:

- How present were you in the passing, the receiving, and the observing?

- Were you breathing?

- Did you connect with the person to whom you were passing and ensure they received your communication, or did you shy away from authentically connecting to the recipient out of embarrassment or uncertainty?

- Did you listen and stay present to the person passing to you and fully receive what they passed or did you presume the gesture based on what you had witnessed going around the circle, i.e., did you communicate the message you received or did you communicate the message you assumed?

- Did you rush the steps of connecting, receiving, connecting, passing?

- It was all the same gesture. Did we all do it the same way?

- Did one person's gesture have more value that the other or were they all equally valuable in their unique way?

Bringing the breath, movement, and vibration to the body is a conscious process of confronting old habits, inhibiting those habits, and introducing new habits through the process of conscious redirection. We know how to breathe, walk, and talk. Or at least we assume we do. We do it serviceably, but we do it unconsciously. Coming back to a neutral body and rebuilding optimal habits of use will prime your body to express confident behaviors in the most authentic way possible.

Playful Practice

What happens when you approach the threshold of fear? When you are called to rise to the occasion, do you advance or retreat? How does that show up in your body? Priming the body to have access to breath and expression is fundamental to meeting this moment with surrender and commitment. What allows you to surrender and commit is play. Inviting play as a practice trains your body to contend with unanticipated moments with a sense of agility and adaptability.

Play is cultivating the land right outside of your comfort zone.

In the previous chapter, you learned to roll down through your spine and find stillness. Play is what fills the stillness with aliveness. Maybe it felt safe to roll through the spine, possibly similar to something you had tried in a yoga class, but it likely didn't feel so outside of your comfort zone that you resisted the exercise entirely. Remember, baby steps. The practices we explore in the following exercises will test the boundaries of your comfort zone. In order to truly engage in the practices, you must harness complete willingness to look and feel silly. There is no actual danger involved here, but your body will respond as such. One of the primary pursuits in the practice of play is a relinquishing of control—physically and vocally. This does not mean you are out of control of basic decency, acting like some reckless jerk making their way down the street, stealing kids' ice cream, and hurting the feelings of the ones you love. It just means you will have greater ease in making elective eye contact with strangers or speaking up in a lively debate.

Play is about teaching your body to shift the narrative from "I couldn't possibly" to "I wonder what would happen if…"

The first three exercises are for your own playful exploration. I want to make sure you feel comfortable playing with yourself before sending you off to play with others. Maintain a lens of observation and an openness to redirection. How are you limiting your expressive potential? How can you do less to allow for more?

BODY

CRAZY 8S →

This is a classic icebreaker exercise for improvisation. I use it in workshops for groups all over the world. It is democratic in its ability to open and avail the participants to vocal expression, movement, and presence. After we do the exercise as a group to kick off our session, I always ask one question in reflection, "How did that feel?" The responses are incredible. These are responses from a workshop I hosted virtually and echo what I hear consistently from other groups:

"It feels so good to MOVE!"

"I need to do this every hour, every day while at the office. WOOOOO!"

"Good vulnerability exercise, haha."

"Play is something we don't do nearly enough of as adults."

"Alive."

The exercise progresses quickly. The purpose of the condition of speed is that it prevents the control- or result-oriented mind from overriding the exploratory body. If you feel super awkward doing this by yourself, pop on your favorite song. If you need a bit more direction, I took the liberty of doing a YouTube search. There are a bunch of weird hits when you just search Crazy 8s, so make sure you include the word "improv." You'll find something there to follow along with. Think about it like a workout video to play.

1. The physical order is right arm, left arm, right leg, left leg.

    a. *I want to emphasize that if you have physical limitations, this exercise can still be effective with just one arm or leg or just the voice. The commitment to the gesture and release of voice and the pace are the most important elements.*

2. You will start by shaking each limb eight times in the above order. For example, shake your right arm quickly eight times while counting out loud up to 8, then your

left arm eight times, your right leg (mind your balance) eight times, and same with your left leg.

3. Then you repeat the pattern, but only count up to seven for each limb.

4. This cycle repeats, one less number each time, until you make your way to one shake for each limb.

5. After one cycle has completed, you will jump and yell, "Woohoo!"

6. The entire process should take no longer than two minutes. Don't ever tell me you don't have time to play!

This exercise will feel really dumb if you don't commit. You will invite too much space for judgment on the practice rather than committing to the practice itself. Commit fully physically. That means you must feel the full extension and expression of the movement, from the shoulder blade all the way through the tips of the fingers. Your arm is like a whip. Commit fully vocally. That means using full vibration and filling the space with your resonance. You will get winded. It is an exertive exercise. Pro tip: Don't eat Chipotle right before.

BIG BODY LITTLE BODY →

I offer this exercise to my private clients to explore after they complete the voice and body practice. The rolling down through the spine, and the muscles and bones, and the order and organization to the practice can feel technical and hyper-focused. This exercise serves to shake up that focus and catapult the practitioner into presence. The exercise is hinged on honoring your impulse to begin, the feeling of readiness experienced in the moment before.

1. Start standing in a space free of obstacles, i.e., low ceilings, lots of delicate sculptures, narrow walls. You want to enter into the moment of expression, unencumbered.

2. Still on your feet, tuck yourself into a little ball. Wrapping your arms around your knees, tucking your head down, squeezing your face. KEEP BREATHING.

3. Repeat the word little to yourself, in your head, quickly. Little, little, little, little, little, etc. This will result in a roller coaster effect, that moment as you ascend to the top of the roller coaster before you come blasting down at full speed.

4. As you are feeling the tension mount and a desire to release build, you will feel a strong desire to release the tension and expand. You will do so by exploding open the body into a starfish shape.

5. Your arms will be extended wide above your head. Your feet will be in a wide stance. Your face will be big, and your tongue extended outside the mouth. KEEP BREATHING.

6. You will feel the expression of the impulse begin to fade and the body moves from expression to holding or wanting to relax. Immediately, condense back into a little body.

7. Repeat two or three times or really as many as you want because it's fun.

8. There is no call for vocalization in this exercise, just presence of breath. However, if you feel inspired to vocalize, I encourage you to do so.

The commitment part is the thing to exercise here. When you feel the big body impulse mount, the spark of yes, honor it. It is about saying *yes* to what your body wants and listening to the call of desire. You want to speak up, go for it. You want to set boundaries, let it out. You want to congratulate a total stranger on the success you just overheard while eavesdropping, do it! Listen to that call for big body activation and catapult yourself across the threshold. This is conscious redirection through play.

VOICE

The following exercise is play for your voice. One of the ways we can strategically influence our audience through play is by using the power of tone and voice. The only way this will be accessible to us is if we cultivate what is called a dynamic range. For example, if you want to shift between scolding (a stronger, deeper, more direct tone) and flirting (a softer, higher pitched, more enchanting tone) with ease, your voice needs to be able to express each of those actions (scolding and flirting) with the appropriate vocal quality. In the last chapter, you activated vibration. This exercise brings vibration to life and offers you a simple way to explore how vibration feels as it shifts through different areas of resonance. Think low to high and everything in between.

LIP BUZZ →

1. You can be standing or seated for this exercise.

2. Place your lips together. You will engage the corners of your mouth just enough to provide stability once the breath is released through the lips.

3. Breathe in deeply through the mouth (into the belly, not the chest!) and release the breath easily. Inhibit any desire to tense the belly or push the air out. That overactivation will prevent the lips from moving.

4. The release of breath will cause the closed lips to flutter together in a buzz-like way. Do this a few times just with the breath to get the feeling of the buzzing action.

5. If you are curious to play with breath control, you can count to ten as you breathe out with a lip buzz. See if you can make it to ten with ease. If not, observe your use and redirect to where you can do less.

6. Once you have gotten the hang of the lip buzz on breath, we will then introduce vibration.

7. Simply, without any constraint, play around with expressing vibration paired with the lip buzz. Maybe that's just moving up and down. You may notice your belly wanting to tense up or your mouth getting tight. Redirect these activations toward release.

8. Intentional vocal play in service of cultivating a dynamic range starts with your finger. You will use your finger as a marker of progress. Start low, go high, and back down again. You are drawing an arch with your finger. Your vibration will follow this path.

9. Your vibration will begin in the chest resonator, make its way through the hard palate (roof of the mouth) and the sinuses, flow through the mask (the third eye region), make its way all the way up into the skull, and back down again. If you feel it is difficult to access the skull resonator (the bright, shiny tones), take your time. It is an underutilized resonator, and the pathway to access it is likely overgrown or blocked. Without forcing the vibration to move

into the skull, ground more deeply in the breath, envision the vibration moving effortlessly upward, and allow the flow of vibration to find its way authentically and effortlessly. Speaking should be as easy as breathing.

10. Taking a deep breath into the belly, release the breath on the exhale and allow the vibration to initiate on the breath wave. Your directing finger starts at the bottom of the arch and moves up as the vibration moves. Ultimately, you will make a complete arch, with the finger ending at the bottom of the arch.

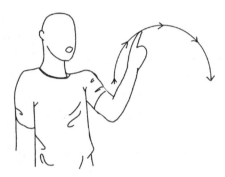

Maybe you nail it right out of the gate. Don't allow that to dissuade you from continuing to practice, and if you are not able to complete the arch on your first try, don't allow that to discourage you from continuing to explore. The finger serves as a gauge of progress as well as an accountability tool. If you only make it halfway up the first part of the arch before losing breath or faltering on vibration, fear not! Now you know exactly where you are and can continue to play around with how to advance your progress through the entire vocal arch. This will allow you to have all the colors of expression available to you and all the notes of a dynamic range so you can effectively play the music of your thoughts.

WORDS
When you move to communicate a thought, that thought must first be met with a vibration that travels through the mouth. Once it crosses the threshold of the mouth, that thought has now become a thing. It is substantive both in perceived vibration and through the experience of the listener. It is the threshold of the mouth that is your moment of choice. Once your thought leaves your mouth, you can no longer make decisions about it. You can be strategic and deliberate in how you move your thoughts with mindful articulation and intentional vocal choices. This is the essence of emotional intelligence and your most powerful tool for creating influence through your speech—the ability to play the music of your thoughts.

We will use the following tongue twister in two distinct ways: for speech and for vocal play.

Peter piper, the pickled pepper picker, picked a peck of pickled peppers. A peck of pickled peppers did Peter Piper the pickled pepper picker pick. Now if Peter Piper, the pickled pepper picker, picked a peck of pickled peppers, where is the peck of pickled peppers that Peter Piper, the pickled pepper picker, picked?

SPEECH →

Speech, the actual execution of sounds, is broken down into two general categories: vowels and consonants. Speech requires activation of your entire face, primarily the muscles around the mouth, along with the tongue and teeth. For this exercise, we will focus on activating the facial muscles in exaggerated ways and highly articulating all the consonant sounds. Consonant sounds are the structure of words. They are the action sounds. They are precise and distinct.

1. Read the tongue twister once just to familiarize yourself with the text. Beware the misconception that tongue twisters must be fast right off the bat. The slower you go, the faster you get there. Slow down.

2. Read it a second time with full intention of exaggerating the facial movements–raising the eyebrows, opening the mouth wide, engaging the smile lines, etc. KEEP BREATHING.

3. Read it a third time with full intention of pronouncing every consonant sound. Feel the movement of your tongue, your tongue making contact with your teeth, or your lips coming together and popping apart. Pay specific attention to the final consonants. Hint: picked ends with a T sound, pickled ends with a D sound.

4. Read it a fourth time and try to incorporate facial movements and precise articulation all together.

5. Repeat.

VOICE →

In this section, we will explore the voice through tactics or mini actions such as tickle, taunt, seduce, or demand. These will anchor you to a point of view and allow you to commit to the voice in a way that has intention and meaning. We activate mini actions intuitively anyway, here we are simply breaking it down to a functional practice. We will also play with the vowel sounds. Vowels are unstructured sounds, which means the voice flows out of the mouth, unimpeded by your lips, tongue, or teeth. Vowels are where the emotion of words are held. Vowels can be lengthened or shortened to convey feeling and point of view.

What you see below is a speaking score. The capitalized words are emphasized words. There are mini actions, shown in (parentheses) throughout, that require specific vocal choices, driven by action and intention. There are also places where the vowels are extended, shown through the use of repeated letters.

Peeeeeter piper, (insinuate) the pickled pepper picker, PICKED a peck of PICKLED peppers. (speculate) A PECK of piiiiiiickled peppers DID Peter Piper the pickled pepper picker PICK. Noooooow IF Peter Piper, (accuse) the pickled pepper picker, (flirt) picked a peck of pickled peppers, WHERE IS the peck of pickled peppers that Peter Piper, the pickled pepper picker, (challenge) picked?

Ultimately, you will put both voice and speech together and play the music of Peter Piper. Go off script. Use the speaking score as a prompt but honor any impulse to deviate. The idea is just to play. No one is watching. Get weird with yourself.

ZIP ZAP ZOP (TO BE PLAYED WITH FRIENDS!)

This is a classic icebreaker exercise that carries a lot of bang for your buck and is just good old-fashioned fun. The important practice here is agility. Unlike the group exercise in the previous chapter, this does not have a predictable flow around a circle. Participants must be in a state of readiness to receive a pass and pass it along at any moment. The game moves quickly in service of keeping everyone on their toes. This game is all about commitment. It requires a commitment to listening, to staying present, to communicating fully and intentionally, and to holding an awareness of what is going on around you while keeping your eye on the ball.

1. This exercise needs at least four participants and should not exceed twenty for optimal game play. Everyone starts by standing in a circle.

2. The exercise incorporates three layers of communication: verbal, nonverbal, and eye contact. The three words (verbal) are Zip, Zap, and Zop. They will always be shared in that order. The gesture to go along with the word (nonverbal) is a clap of the hands pointed toward the person to whom they are passing. The connection to the person to whom they are passing (eye contact) serves as the agreement for receiving, i.e., "I see you. Here you go."

3. To begin, everyone needs to assume a stance of readiness. As people are standing in the circle, arms will be crossed, legs will be crossed, attention will wander. Call everyone to attention and get them in their bodies. I like to bring them into a football stance—into the lower body, knees bent, hands up, ready to catch the ball.

4. One person begins by connecting to someone across the circle, passing Zip paired with the gesture and eye contact.

5. The person who receives the Zip immediately moves to connect with someone else through eye contact and passes a Zap with the gesture.

6. The person who receives the Zap follows the same pattern of connecting but passes a Zop.

7. This pattern repeats itself (Zip, Zap, Zop) until someone (inevitably) messes up by not paying attention, passing without making the agreement and resulting in a fumble, or saying the wrong word, at which point everyone in the circle cheers to celebrate the failure and you start again.

8. Repeat as many times as you like.

Everything we have addressed in this chapter comes down to one important fact: there is always opportunity to play. We can play with how sounds come out of our mouth. We can play with the placement and amplification of vibration in the body. We can play with the expansiveness of our bodies and the expressiveness of our impulse. There will never be a time when you cannot take into consideration how you wish to play the game. This is always within your control. When approaching the threshold of fear, rather than retreating, how can you encourage yourself to make a strategic decision, to lower the stakes on failure and simply make a choice to adapt, to commit fully to something that feels uncomfortable, to Zap to someone's Zip?

A Playful Life

———

Joseph Campbell, one of the greatest American masters of story, once wrote that our purpose in speaking is to "communicate directly from one inward world to another, in such a way that an actual shock of experience will have been rendered: not a mere statement for the information or persuasion of a brain, but an effective communication across the void of space and time from one center of consciousness to another." (AZ Quotes) Pause. Go back and read that again.

When we perceive confidence, this is the experience we have. We are penetrated. We are touched. We are linked to the messenger because the messenger is committed to connecting with us. In a confident body, you are not building relationships on a mere statement for the brain. You are speaking to be felt. If you're not speaking to be felt, put it in an email.

When do you feel most alive? Those moments when you are not thinking, you're simply responding, in harmony with your environment. You are open to laughter, honest conversation, and deep listening. Your body and breath are behind you in that experience. You have surrendered to immediacy and presence. You are in the landscape of the NOW, unburdened by consequence or propriety. Yet somehow you almost always manage to stay safe, respect others, and leave the interaction unscathed. Entering a space of play and presence, does not mean leaving propriety at home. All can coexist.

The key is to care deeply but not give a shit.

Caring deeply means having compassion and consideration for the world around you. Caring about the outcomes and impact on others. Not giving a shit is about healing the relationship between you and your ego. When you communicate, especially in public speaking, it can be easy to make it about you and doing a good job or saying the right thing. But it's never about you, and there is no guaranteed right thing. Your ego is safe. You are free to play.

One of the biggest blockers I witness when it comes to crossing the threshold of fear, beyond our physical resistance, is the attachment to saying the right thing in the right way. We are so concerned with saying the right thing, yet harbor little consideration for the meaning or the impact of those words on our listener. We think about what the listener will think about what we're saying, but not enough about what our listener will feel. We are attached to words as somehow representative of our capability, credibility, and value. If we say the wrong thing, we will be judged, ridiculed, and rejected. What if, instead, we direct our attention to how we say things instead of what we are saying? This will result in a liberated relationship to communication.

We are fixated on words as the primary mechanism for getting our message across and believing that what is said is the most important element in inspiring the world to listen. This holds us hostage in our heads and inhibits speaking from our hearts. If our hearts, our truth, our authenticity are driving our communication, if our voice and body are present in the communication, then our words are of little consequence. Our listener will feel and experience our truth. They will be the recipient of our authentic vibration. They will feel our words, not just hear our words.

When we speak, only 7 percent of what the audience receives is verbal. The remaining 93 percent is nonverbal.

Yet we place a disproportionate amount of energy of the what over the how. If you give yourself permission to surrender attachment to the words and redirect your presence to the voice, the connection, and the intention, you will feel a revitalized experience in making yourself heard. Use your voice, not your words. This invites play.

I was hosting a two-day training for a foundation in Sao Paulo, Brazil. The participants were emerging leaders and early professionals. They were high performers, well educated, and deeply committed to doing good work. They spoke Portuguese as their first language and business English. We had translators on site to assist in the training. One of the primary objectives for the training was to enhance presentation skills and executive presence. The participants were asked to present in English, since much of their work was about nurturing relationships with policy makers and researchers in the US. Despite how capable these young professionals were, they were so attached to saying things correctly that they lost all sense of presence and play in the process. I had a solution.

I introduced an exercise called "Expert Translator." This was with no intention of irony, given our two translators in the room. The exercise goes like this: Two people volunteer to come to the front of the room. One is designated expert, and the other is designated translator. The trick is that the expert is from a land unknown (Narnia, for example) and speaks a language unfamiliar to the group (gibberish). This is why it's very fortunate that they have brought their translator. The audience picks a topic for the expert (mating rituals among sea horses in space, for example). The expert then proceeds to give an improvised presentation on this topic in their native tongue (again, gibberish). The translator then translates the presentation simultaneously so the audience can understand. This is then followed with an improvised Q&A where the translator has to communicate back to the expert using their native language (gibberish).

A few predictable patterns emerge. The person playing the expert feels ridiculous speaking gibberish at first, demonstrating deep attachment to words as their primary mode for communicating their message. This results in a disconnection from their body and freedom of vocal expression. You can also witness a delay in their communication as they attempt to translate the words in their head into gibberish, placing the entire responsibility to convey meaning on the words they are saying. Eventually, they surrender to the game. They experience freedom in a detachment from words and a liberation in committing to the tone, the gesture, and the body language. The person operating as translator is initially trying to make a literal translation from gibberish into something coherent based on what they think the other person is saying. Eventually, they relax into the realization that they can make up whatever words they want and simply receive the experts' "language" as points of inspiration, rather than rigid guidelines.

See, what was missing in the more traditional presentation skills assessment, where they were trapped within a system of imposed expectation and performance guidelines, was the participants' willingness to surrender to the moment, to be carried by the how rather than the what. They were speaking from the head and not the heart. After playing "Expert Translator," there was a collective experience of release and a higher threshold for imperfection, presence, and authentic expression. The game brought them back to life.

Our attachment to language is limiting. It limits our freedom of expression, and it limits our ability to connect. How many times have you been thinking about what you're going to say as someone is speaking to you? What if I told you that you never have to predetermine your words if you are connected to the intention behind your intuitive thought? Everything you need to know in order to respond, exists outside of your head. It is found in the space of active listening.

One of the most important tools that will allow you to engage in all the functional behaviors of confidence as well as grant your ego permission to surrender to the unknown of any given interaction, is the tool of YES, AND. This is a foundational tool of improvisation and a surprising tool for confident communication. I touched on it briefly in a previous chapter but will take a deeper dive here.

YES, AND is a method of cueing your brain to respond to what was just said instead of feeling a burden to generate a brand-new idea. It will cultivate the habit of active listening because you can't respond to what was just said if you're not paying attention. It will give you a simple prompt to contribute to conversations with an individual or a group. It is a formula that allows you to play well with others.

The three components of YES, AND are acknowledge, elevate, and advance. The YES says I hear you and have received what you just said. The AND is the transition word that leads to an elevation or deepening of the other person's contribution. This elevation then advances the conversation forward with an experience of collaboration and co-creation. Play is no fun if you only hear NO or YES, BUT. The interplay and exchange are lost.

YES, AND keeps a conversation alive. It invites imagination and connection.

You can use it explicitly. This means intentionally incorporating the words "yes, and" into your responses. For example, your boss says, "I think this new initiative is lacking finesse," to which you respond, "Yes, and what a wonderful opportunity to gain collective clarity on what we are working toward." This explicit incorporation will be a valuable strategy especially as you are beginning to explore this technique. It will consciously develop and reinforce the habit of active listening and authentic response in replace of the desire to "say the right thing." You can also use it as an internal calibration tool without saying the actual words. It challenges you to consider if you are acknowledging what the other person has just said and if you are seeking to advance or deny their contribution. This is really about ensuring that each person feels seen and heard, while making interacting a little easier and likely more enjoyable, even in challenging conversations.

Here's a totally made up (and likely scientifically inaccurate) example of an improvisation exercise I teach in my workshops called "What's in the Box?"

Person A - What's in the box?

Person B - A baby turtle.

Person A - Yes, and that turtle looks like it can't be more than a couple days old.

Person B - Yes, and you can tell their age by the maturing of the color on their shells.

Person A - Yes, and I see there are darker spots coming in near the turtle's head.

Person B - Yes, and those spots will continue to flow toward the tail.

Person A doesn't know what's in the box, so they have to respond to whatever Person B says is in the box. In life, we rarely know what's in the box either. The two players then YES, AND at every exchange, co-creating an imaginary dialogue. This same framework can be applied to nearly any interaction in which you find yourself and is especially helpful during first meetings or interactions, as well as in brainstorm sessions or projects requiring teamwork.

In practice, play can be a powerful tool for our most high-stakes moments.

Play supports us moving through moments of uncertainty or when we are engaging in a challenging conversation. It doesn't diminish the gravity of any circumstance or make light of meaningful moments. Again, play is not unserious. It is a tool. It allows you to navigate situations strategically and embody those actions authentically. Play promotes healthy competition and critical discourse rather than a toxic "win at all costs" dynamic. There isn't fighting to dominate and eliminate the adversary. It allows you to pursue an objective with full commitment, but still congratulate your opponent if you lose. The actor playing Claudius doesn't leave the stage ready to murder the actor playing Hamlet. He played the actions of the character fully and now he and his fellow actors go out for beers.

Next time you find yourself in a heated argument, for example, what happens if you intentionally shift your vocal tone and adjust your body positioning? What if, instead of defending yourself or asserting your point of view, you engaged with a YES, AND mindset? What impact does that have on the other person? Notice and respond. That is play. It's listening, observing, and responding. It's not making light of. It's sincere as hell.

Play is not only effective for conversation or unplanned moments. Play can be practically applied to the process of preparation. For example, when my clients begin the process of designing and delivering a keynote, I always encourage them to initiate the process out loud and on their feet. Not only does this allow for movement and activation of the breath, which gets the brain flowing, it also builds muscle memory around the flow of the talk and allows authentic language to emerge rather than an intellectualized version of the thought they would ideally like to have. The content will take on a consistent form while removing a need to script or memorize. The content, developed through impulse and intuition connected to the breath, takes on a characteristic of aliveness and immediacy, even though it is planned and prepared.

The development process starts with talking through the main points out loud up to five times, taking notes as necessary. Then move to write it down into a cohesive structure and attend to narrative flow. You can also refer to this as a skeleton outline or a list of sequential talking points. Once the flow is tweaked and nuanced, practice begins. Practice also happens out loud and on your feet with the added condition of dynamic movement and vocalization. This will feel silly. You cannot practice in polished form or in service of perfection, which, as a reminder, does not exist in the realm of human behavior. You must practice with free movement of body and voice first; gain familiarity with the flow of the content on its feet and in your voice. Then you can start to polish through establishing blocking zones for intentional movement and incorporate any tech that may be present, such as a slide deck or microphone. I always like to say, "I am a great singer... in my head."

You can never perform at your highest if you don't prepare with muscle memory in mind. Communication is a physical activity. Play first. Polish second.

You can invite others to play with you through establishing rules of the game. We can see the benefit of this directly in our virtual meetings. How do we all play well together if we don't know what the rules are? When can I speak? How do I communicate? Is it a free for all or do we raise our hand? Coming into a meeting with an intention for flow and achievement of a desired outcome will set the stage for success, allow all the players to perform at higher levels, and offer a sense of safety in service of surrender and connection. In personal relationships, you can establish rules for communication and boundaries. This allows everyone to know when they can play together, when they need to play alone, and when someone else can challenge them to play in a different way.

If you have never taken an improv class, do that. If you can't remember the last time you cried from laughing, surround yourself with the people who are most likely to bring that out in you. If you watch and rarely participate, YES, AND your way in and be open to surprising yourself. Practice and all is coming.

I worked with the general manager of a luxury hotel brand who was terrified of speaking in public. He was such a charming, charismatic person. He had no trouble building relationships or acting from a space of authenticity, unless he had to present to a large group. He was fixated on words and how he would be received. He was set to deliver a rebranding speech that presented a revived vision for the hotel, as well as revised values for the corporate culture. He wanted to do a "good job" and that intention was undermining his ability to do so. He was practicing toward perfection, rather than possibility.

The solution? A trampoline. His desire to be dynamic and present during his presentation was there, but his body was against him. He was holding his breath, and all of a sudden, he had no idea what to do with his hands. I asked him to buy a mini trampoline and directed that we would spend the majority of our practice time bouncing while speaking. This brought him out of his head, into his body, and into a landscape of play rather than perfection. He connected his words to feelings and intention rather than as mere statements for the information of the brain.

I had another client who was an ad sales account executive for a media company. One of her primary responsibilities was to pitch new clients. She came to me because she had identified that she was losing motivation and influence. Her numbers had dropped over the previous two-quarters, and she was ready to take action. Our first session, I asked her to present her deck from her most recent pitch. It was fine, but not alive. I learned that the deck they used was a template and although customized for each client, had remained relatively unchanged for years. There was a recommended flow and talking points that had been established before she was in the role, so she was speaking from a deck and system that didn't represent her authentic form of communication.

The solution? Storytelling. The deck she was using was chocked full of data, analytics, and return rates, but devoid of imagination or opportunity to influence the listener with language of possibility. I had her present the deck using only stories. This meant when she wanted to highlight a data point, she had to share it in a way that spoke to the why over the what. Stories speak to our hearts, not just our heads and therefore are more likely to gain the trust and attention from your audience. Effective storytelling also requires surrendering to the imagination and inviting dynamic tone and emotionality. The notion of going off script was revolutionary for her. The idea of bringing in storytelling was what brought her back to life.

YES, AND is a philosophy, not just a communication tool. It is a way to say yes to life, take risks, and embrace moments when you may have a tendency to retreat rather than advance. I have built my life on the philosophy of YES, AND. It was my post-marriage mindset shift. I had deviated from my expected path and was in unknown territory. I could have stagnated. I could have simply survived. But instead, I chose to operate intentionally with YES, AND, and it has allowed me to lead an incredible life.

I said YES, AND to going to India for a month even though I was broke and had no itinerary other than get to Mysore to practice ashtanga yoga and travel around. I found myself in a mountain town in Southern India called Ooty, in a hotel room that was pulled straight from a David Lynch film with green carpeted walls and a door that led to nowhere. I said YES, AND when my partner at the time approached me after getting off a very expensive phone call with his parents to share that his mom had been diagnosed with pancreatic cancer. I said YES, AND to his desire to stay in India for the remainder of our journey, knowing that his mother was weeks away from death. I said YES, AND when, after five years together, he determined that he needed a fresh start, leaving me having to say YES, AND to living alone and supporting myself for the first time in my adult life.

I said YES, AND to going on a two-week sailing adventure with a relative stranger because I trusted my intuition of safety, I calculated the risk, and assessed the potential for reward. There was no working bathroom, no running water, and no working kitchen. We cooked on a Coleman gas stove, used a bucket for a bathroom, and washed dishes from a solar shower bag. We also saw breathtaking sunsets, made friends with dolphins, laughed and laughed, and rediscovered our relationship to silence. It wound up being the trip that transformed the way I design my life.

I said YES, AND to writing this book. To dedicating the time, mental capacity, and emotional bandwidth to bring this message of confidence to you.

Imagine a life led with NO. A life of negating the moment. A life of resisting play. Now imagine a life where you make the decision to say YES, AND. A life driven by the question, "I wonder what would happen if..." Play takes risk. It takes courage. A confident body is a body open to excellence and failure equally and at all times. Play will add the layer of resilience needed to carry forth and continue the work. This is within your control. We are all capable of living in a confident body.

CONCLUSION

CONCLUSION

No Dumb Questions

There is no such thing as a dumb question.

First of all, I am always an advocate for coming back to basics and clarifying foundation before diving deeper into any practice. Oftentimes, we assume we know things because they are so rudimentary that how could we not. However, like losing our connection to breath even though we "do it all the time," it is remarkably easy to lose presence and knowledge around behaviors like listening, body awareness, and being present to the thoughts that are coming out of your mouth.

Second, I am certain there is at least one other person who has the same question, and you are now the hero for asking. Assumption is the most toxic ingredient to confident behavior. We spent a tremendous amount of time on the practice of observation because it is so easy to assume rather than confirm. If you don't know something or have uncertainty around a basic idea, there is likely a lack of clarity in the delivery of the direction or information offered and/or an opportunity to limit the potential for assumption. Never be afraid to clarify or ask the most obvious thing.

As you made your way through these chapters, gaining deeper understanding around how you can develop behaviors of confidence, you may be sincerely inspired, but also have a presentation on Tuesday and seriously just need some tips for how to navigate in the immediate terms. Lasting transformation is ideal but takes time (perhaps a lifetime). For the moments where you don't have the time to let transformation take hold and need a simple tip or tool, I give you the answers to the "dumb" questions:

How do I stop being nervous?

Make friends with nerves. They matter. You cannot stop being nervous. Stopping is resisting or dismissing. It's similar to the "visiting forces." Welcome the nerves as new information. Don't try to get rid of your nerves. Allow your nerves to flow through you. When you are feeling what is typically expressed as nervousness, it is actually your body preparing to rise to the occasion. It is your body preparing to step deeply into action and presence. The adrenaline you feel can feel like the experience of nervousness but is an energy source that will allow you to hold the attention of your audience and speak with power. It is your fuel for influence.

If you feel the nervousness overwhelming you, get back into your body and release energy to bring you back to presence. Releasing energy can look like a full-body shakeout, a lip buzz, bouncing around, or releasing the voice. If you are caught in your nervous narrative, you must free the body of holding and tension. Nervousness will likely move you into your head and out of your breath. Come back to your body, connect to your WHY, and continue with presence.

What do I do with my hands?

The central idea around what I will suggest is that your hand should always be available to gesture. This means they cannot be tightly held together, crossed and locked, or clenched behind your back. The other side of this is, you want to ensure your hands aren't distracting and extraneously moving all over the place. Remember that confidence implies we are open to movement without the continuous desire to move. This applies to the hands as well.

You want your hands to support your thoughts through aligned movement and visual representation. For example, when counting through a list (this thing, this other thing, and this final thing—using fingers to punctuate the items on the list).

When your hands are not serving to support your message, keep them at home base. Home base is hands lightly folded right above your belly button or at the solar plexus. It's like you're holding a tiny baby chicken. Don't squeeze your hands too tightly or the chicken gets squished. Elbow are bent nice and soft at your sides at a relative ninety-degree angle. Your shoulders are dropped, and you have a little bubble of space in the armpits. This last bit is important. If you are clenching in your armpits, your gesture will be lost, and it will compromise your breath. In fact, armpits are the most important element when referring to gesture.

This hand positioning will apply for formal and informal moments of interaction and are doubly important during virtual interaction. You can use the home base position at a bar as democratically as you can in a boardroom. It's a neutral position that keeps you soft, feels a bit safe, and sets you up to incorporate gesture when it's called for. For virtual use of gesture, you will have to make sure your gesture enters into the screen. It is vital information to your audience, so you need to make sure they can see you. This will feel weird since you will likely have to bring your hands slightly higher than feels natural.

To practice what to do with your hands, observe your natural instinct. Are you an enthusiastic hand talker? Do you tend to keep your hands out of the process all together? If you tend to overuse your hands (indicated by not using them intentionally), then practice speaking to someone while sitting on your hands. You will notice how often you go to tug your hands from under you and begin to modify the habit simply through awareness. If you don't use your hands at all, practice speaking to someone with a broad gesture. This will seem organic if you use them when emphasizing or when referring to something explicit. For example, "Oh right! (gesture with both hands open) You mentioned (point at the person) that that other person (point elsewhere to indicate someone else) wasn't coming." Applying this to more formal speaking, you want to keep home base consistently engaged. It will give the impression of polish. You will intuitively notice where your gesture seeks to support your point. Identify these consciously and incorporate deliberately, almost like blocking, as you practice your speech or presentation.

Where should I be looking when I present or speak in public?

The first thing to note here is that no matter where you are looking, make sure you are actually registering the world outside of yourself. See your audience; don't just look at them. This will keep you present, in your body, and out of your head.

When we talk about where to look, we are actually talking about points of focus. This may mean deliberately making eye contact within a smaller group (a meeting with your team or at a bar with two friends). This may also mean simply landing your gaze at deliberate points in the space when speaking to large groups (a pitch competition or a wedding toast). Landing your gaze and making eye contact are the same thing in terms of impact. When you are looking at something specific outside of yourself, it will ground you. If you are washing your gaze (not landing on anything specific), you will feel a distinct lack of clarity in your mind and flow of thoughts. This will activate or increase anxiety. Speaking to something or someone specific will allow your thoughts to land with intention. Speaking to a general something will create unspecific cognitive processing, you will lose your train of thought, and your audience will feel disconnected.

Suggested map for where to look:

A small group -

Make authentic eye contact with your listener. Hold for about two beats (bum-bum), and then shift your focus to another person or avert eye contact for a moment and return to that person. Keep breathing.

A large group -

Identify three points of focus that are somewhere between the front and the back of the room and are spaced out equally from right to left of the room. These will be your landing points as you move between thoughts or in the middle of a thought. For example:

"What happens when we shift our gaze (shift focal point) is that our audience is able to follow the flow of thoughts (shift focal point). That is to the benefit of everyone (pause, zoom out, see the entire space, land focus back on one point, continue) including yourself."

What happens when I forget what I am saying or lose my train of thought?

If you have lost your train of thought, the larger recommendation is to reflect on how you prepared to speak and how present and invested you were in communicating your message. Was your focus on being heard or just talking to get through your thought? Are you speaking at someone or are you speaking to them? This will have a dramatic effect on your ability to stay connected to how your thoughts move into words.

Other possible reasons you forget what you're saying are that you are feeling overwhelmed in other aspects of your life, distracted by something outside of the topic at hand, tired, hungry, thirsty, the list goes on. There are a number of reasons why you may be losing your train of thought, but all of them reflect on your level of presence and connection to your breath for both communication and active listening. If you're not breathing, your brain will stop working.

When you notice you have lost your train of thought, pause and come back to this moment. This can happen in a split second. It's like when you're driving and all of a sudden you realize you've been driving for several minutes and are not conscious of it. Presence is not a permanent state of being. It comes and goes, sometimes at inopportune moments like the middle of a high-stakes public presentation. Reconnect with your audience. If it feels authentic to verbally acknowledge your lost thought (without apologizing, but rather honoring the blissful moment of human imperfection), then I encourage you to do so. "Hah, I was talking and all of a sudden, I forgot what I was going to say. Does that ever happen to you? Anyway, what I was saying was..." This is the invitation of play and expression of authenticity. The fun is in the flaw. No one pays to see perfect.

If you realize you are in the middle of speaking and have lost your point, use this simple phrase to cue your brain to get back on track and wrap it up:

"So that's why I _____."

It sounds crazy, but it works every time for both prepared and extemporaneous speech.

How do I move when speaking in public?

Less is more when it comes to movement. By encouraging your body to embrace stillness, you limit the potential for aimless wandering. Unspecific movement leads to an unspecific delivery of a message. When embracing stillness, make sure you are avoiding stiffness. You need to be available to movement and stiffness will prevent the flow from happening and authentic expression from emerging organically.

Incorporate the tool of blocking zones. I have touched on this in previous chapters and will expand on it here. This will apply to virtual speaking as well. It's all about creating distinct places to shift your body that echo a shift in content. Define three zones. If you are on a stage, the zones will be wider spaced, spanning the width of the stage. If you are virtual, the zones will be tighter and closer in proximity, since you have a much smaller frame of movement.

Standing center, look at the floor in front of you. That is Zone 1. To your left is Zone 2 and to your right is Zone 3. Start in Zone 1. Stand still, connect to your audience, and tell the truth. Complete the thought and move to Zone 2 before you start the next thought. Land in Zone 2 and begin your next thought. Continue to move between Zones in relationship to the structure of your thoughts. Move between thoughts. Deliver the thought standing within a zone. This will create a strong visual for the audience and allow you as the speaker to find space and breath between your thoughts as well as ground your body in your message.

Suggested map for where to move:

Introduction of idea – Zone 1 "I am Minna Taylor, and I want to talk to you all about confidence."

Pause (breathe) and move to Zone 2. Land in Zone 2.

A story that illuminates my point – Zone 2 "When I was a little girl…"

Complete the essence of your story. Pause (breathe) and move to Zone 3. Land in Zone 3.

The transition thought from story into presentation of the main idea – Zone 3 "What I discovered was…"

I recommend defining deliberate points to shift zones ahead of time and build this into your practice and preparation. Just like you work to gain familiarity with the content, you must get familiar with the physical flow of the content. Remember that most of what the audience receives is nonverbal and speaking is a physical activity.

How do I know if they like what I am saying?

First, let me ask you this question: If you were in the middle of a presentation and you got the feeling that people didn't like what you were saying, would you stop talking and walk out the door? Probably not. Place your attention elsewhere, like on the things you can control—breath, body, voice.

Second question to consider: Do *you* like what you're saying? Does it matter to you? If you don't care about what you're saying, you shouldn't expect your audience to care either.

Although you can't possibly know with any level of certainty that your audience likes what you're saying, you can tell if they are paying attention. It is your sole job as the speaker to hold the attention of your audience. How they feel or what they think is irrelevant. Whether they are paying attention or not is everything.

If you become aware that you are worried they don't like what you're saying, odds are they have simply stopped paying attention. That is not necessarily a reflection on the appeal of your content, but likely a reflection of your delivery and an internal call to action to dive deeper into presence and release of expression. Remember, we are not just making statements for the information of a brain. If you're not speaking to be heard, put it in an email.

If you start to notice people having side conversations, unsettled rustling in the crowd, phones coming out, etc., that is your cue to reignite presence for yourself and demand the attention of your audience. Deliberately shift your tone or energy of your speaking. Find dynamics in your voice to bring it back to life. Move your body to a different point in the room, sit down, shift levels, shake it up. If you have been locked or flat in your delivery, maybe invite a moment of humanity to come through. Laugh, shift your tone to telling a secret, pause in silence. Start to play the music of your thoughts. Then if they tell you they still didn't like it, at least it will be more enjoyable in the process.

And finally....

What if they don't like me?

What if they do?

Acknowledgments

You are reading this book due to the tremendous efforts of an incredible extended author community. I wrote the book, but it could not have made its way into your hands without the support and advocacy from an incredible group of people.

I would like to thank my dad, Pete, very intentionally. He encouraged me to write a book even before I started writing this book. He was my first beta reader and offered incredibly insightful feedback. He was the first order during my presale campaign. He has remained a champion for the success of the book, and I like to believe he is my very first fan. I love you pop.

Beta Readers
Mary Catherine Bassett
Peter Richardson
Philippe Danielides
Edu van der Werf
Jenne Richardson

Major Gift Donors
Honor Yoga Foundation
John Jay College CUNY
Episcopal Diocese of Long Island

Large Donors
Marissa Badgley
Domenica Stasiak
Gautam Deviah
Jay Biss
Pete Richardson
Allison and Schafer Kowalchik
Brenda Rigney

Author Community Donors
Freya Taylor
Alex Hollywood
Philippe Danielides
Tamara Saleh
Laura Ramadei
Maulik Dave
Sean Harvey
Jess Brain
Juvoni Beckford
Sheila Buckley
Chris Chung
Mary Beth Lacki
Moira Doran
Steve Smith
Javier Valdez
Joe Forish
Lawrese Brown

Thomasina Williams
Jenne Richardson
Christina Singh
Andrew Davies
Shanice Graves
Julie Grega
Miles Cutler
Melanie Harter
Emily Furr
Jen Gitomer
Kelly Benoit
Gee Kay (GK) Cheung
Ezekiel (Zeke) Rutman-Allen
Tim Daoust
Rebecca (Becky) McDougal
Kristen Berke
Far Momin
Emily Rubin
Lindsey Barrow
Jenny Davenport
Marie Petin
Tamara Saleh
Jeffrey Jagling
Edu van der Werf
Jessica Durand Ewton
Olive Persimmon (buy her books too!)
Brandon James Willett
Abigail Lehman
Lindsey Vance
Mint Boonyapanachoti
Marlena Montgomery
Estee Perlmutter

David Munoz
Monica Domantay
Miles Cutler
Christian O'Brien
John Kester
Gautam Deviah
Melissa Shaw
Nikki Thomas
Jeff Chrzan
Randy Kleinman
Jessica Seibert
Kelsey Kirkley
Jamila Diaz
Tammy blank
Miguel Galeano
Flannery Winchester
Serkan Alkan
Sally Chung
Cara Valentino
Mary Bassett
Cesar Vallejo
Ellen M Richardson
Elizabeth Pagedas
Lisa Anderson
Dana Kaplan
Gesche Nemitz
Raul Espinoza
Allison Davis
Lauren Chiarello Mika
Charles Walters
Jennifer Sills
Lloyd Cambridge

Colleen Blum
Michelle Miller
Melek Ozeren
Zayd Sukhun
Sam Haberle
Frederica McLean
Eric Koester (the man, the myth, the legend)

APPENDIX

WELCOME

Brown, Brené. *Dare to Lead.* New York: Random House Publishing, 2018.

Studio Lambert, Producer. *The Circle.* Season 1, episode 1, "Hello, Circle." Aired January 1, 2020, on Netflix.

LEARN

UNCONSCIOUS CONDITIONING

Caprino, Kathy. "The Top Regrets of the Dying and What We Need to Learn from Them." *Forbes,* December 13, 2019. https://www.forbes.com/sites/kathycaprino/2019/12/13/the-top-regrets-of-the-dying-and-what-we-need-to-learn-from-them/?sh=3104b-cd17ce7

Rodenburg, Patsy. *The Right to Speak: Working with the Voice.* New York: Routledge, 1992.

NOW YOU SEE IT

van der Kolk, Bessel. *The Body Keeps the Score: Brain, Mind, and Body in the Healing of Trauma.* New York: Viking Penguin, 2014.

STATUS AND POWER

TEDx Talks. "Don't Do Your Best | Keith Johnstone | TEDxYYC" September 12, 2016. Video, 12:26. https://www.youtube.com/watch?v=bz9mo4qW9bc

WHAT IS POSSIBLE

Habermann, Amanda. "Why We Resist Change: How Behavioral Inertia Affects Success in Exercise and Weight Loss Goals." *The Truisms of Wellness* (Blog). *Psychology Today,* January 25, 2017. https://www.psychologytoday.com/us/blog/the-truisms-wellness/201701/why-we-resist-change.

Oxford Reference. s.v. "The Butterfly Effect." Accessed February 12, 2022. https://www.oxfordreference.com/view/10.1093/oi/authority.20110803095538985

Tippet, Krista. "Sharon Salzberg: The Healing Is in the Return." Updated August 5, 2021. *On Being.* Produced by On Being Studios. Podcast, MP3 audio, 50:53. https://onbeing.org/programs/sharon-salzberg-the-healing-is-in-the-return/

IMAGINE

BENEFITS OF DISCOMFORT

Tolle, Eckhardt. "Transforming Our Consciousness Through Adversity." May 27, 2021. In *Essential Teachings*. Produced by Oprah Winfrey. Podcast, MP3 audio, 33:52. https://www.oprah.com/own-podcasts/transforming-our-consciousness-through-adversity_1

INEVITABLE VULNERABILITY

Harvard Health Publishing. "Giving Thanks Can Make You Happier." *Health Beat,* August 14, 2021. https://www.health.harvard.edu/healthbeat/giving-thanks-can-make-you-happier.

Maslow, Abraham. "A Theory of Human Motivation." *Psychology Review.* 50, 4 (1943): 430–437.

Restrepo, Sandra, dir. *The Call to Courage.* Released April 19, 2019, on Netflix.

Rodenburg, Patsy. *The Second Circle.* New York: W.W. Norton & Company, 2008.

BODY AND BREATH

Ma, Xiao, Zi-Qi Yue, Zhu-Qing Gong, Hong Zhang, Nai-Yue Duan, Yu-Tong Shi, Gao-Zia Wei, You-Fa Li. "The Effect of Diaphragmatic Breathing on Attention, Negative Affect and Stress in Healthy Adults" *Frontiers in Psychology*; 8, (June 6, 2017): 874. 10.3389/fpsyg.2017.00874.

Rifkin, Rachel. "How Shallow Breathing Affects Your Whole Body." *Headspace*. Accessed October 5, 2021. https://www.headspace.com/articles/shallow-breathing-whole-body

AWARENESS

Spielberg, Steven, dir. *Hook*. 1991; Universal City, CA: Amblin Entertainment. Blu-ray Disc, 1080p HD.

Watts, Allen. *The Wisdom of Insecurity: A Message for An Age of Anxiety*. New York: Pantheon Books, 1951.

PLAY

MOVEMENT AND VIBRATION

Johnstone, Keith. *Impro: Improvisation and the Theatre*. London: Faber and Faber LTD, 1979.

Perel, Esther. *Mating in Captivity*. New York: HarperCollins Publishing, 2006.

A PLAYFUL LIFE

AZ Quotes. "Joseph Campbell Quotes." Accessed January 13, 2022. https://www.azquotes.com/quote/808973

Made in the USA
Middletown, DE
18 August 2023